Tahmeed Zaman

The Impending Demise of the Euro

The Impact of Monetary Policy on the Sustainability of the Euro

Anchor Academic
Publishing

Zaman, Tahmeed: The Impending Demise of the Euro. The Impact of Monetary Policy on the Sustainability of the Euro, Hamburg, Anchor Academic Publishing 2017

Buch-ISBN: 978-3-96067-176-3
PDF-eBook-ISBN: 978-3-96067-676-8
Druck/Herstellung: Anchor Academic Publishing, Hamburg, 2017

Bibliografische Information der Deutschen Nationalbibliothek:
Die Deutsche Nationalbibliothek verzeichnet diese Publikation in der Deutschen Nationalbibliografie; detaillierte bibliografische Daten sind im Internet über http://dnb.d-nb.de abrufbar.

Bibliographical Information of the German National Library:
The German National Library lists this publication in the German National Bibliography. Detailed bibliographic data can be found at: http://dnb.d-nb.de

Hermannstal 119k, 22119 Hamburg
http://www.diplomica-verlag.de, Hamburg 2017
Printed in Germany

Abstract

The aim of this thesis is to study the impact of expansionary monetary policy on the European economies through the conceptual framework of the Austrian Business Cycle Theory. The European Central Bank has continually reduced interest rates as a policy measure to counter the sovereign debt crisis and the thesis examines the implications of this venture. From Germany's perspective, the viability of reverting to the Deutschmark in times of monetary instability is also explored. The results, based on the deductive reasoning principle of the Austrian School reveal that a monetary policy aiming for sound money should be implemented with immediate effect. Control of the money supply and credit should be left to the market with no scope for central banks to manipulate the interest rates. The thesis sets forth an agenda whereby Germany should exit the European Monetary Union, but stay in the European Union. The cost of such an exit will impose significant losses on German citizens, but these losses will be much lower, compared to the incalculable risks and costs associated with the euro rescue mission. The findings show that another huge financial crisis is fast approaching, so in terms of limiting the damage, bringing back the Deutschmark and dismantling the single currency altogether may prove to be the best way forward.

Acknowledgements

I would first like to thank my thesis advisor, Professor Dr. Benno Feldmann of the International Business Administration department at Worms University of Applied Sciences. Prof. Feldmann consistently allowed this paper to be my own work, but also steered me in the right direction whenever I required assistance by providing prompt feedback and answering all the questions I had about my research.

I would also like to acknowledge Professor Dr. Olaf Rieck as the second reader of this thesis, and I am indebted to him for his valuable advice.

I take this opportunity to give my heartfelt thanks to Ralitsa Stancheva for an insightful discussion regarding the low interest rates in Europe, which encouraged me to delve deeper into the subject matter. I am also grateful to Christoph Kirsch for going out of his way to provide me with stock market data from Bloomberg, and for several astute conversations that broadened my line of thinking.

A time-sensitive thesis like this is the product of intense work, and it would have been much more difficult without the help of my family members. So finally, I must express profound gratitude to my parents and my sister for providing me with unfailing support and continuous encouragement throughout the time needed for researching and writing the thesis. This accomplishment would not have been possible without them. Thank you!

Table of Contents

List of Abbreviations

ABCT	Austrian Business Cycle Theory
DM	Deutschmark
ECB	European Central Bank
EMU	European Monetary Union
EONIA	Euro Overnight Index Average
ESCB	European System of Central Banks
EU	European Union
Fed	Federal Reserve of the United States
GDP	Gross Domestic Product
OCA	Optimum Currency Area
PIIGS	Portugal, Ireland, Italy, Greece, and Spain
QE	Quantitative Easing
Repo	Repurchase Agreement

List of Tables

List of Figures

Chapter 1: Introduction

The sad reality is that the European countries that currently find themselves submerged in the sovereign debt quagmire are not in a position to get out of it any time soon. It all started when interest rates fell down drastically, encouraging investments and spending that were not backed by an increase in savings. Bastasin (2012) observed that the eurozone had been on the verge of sinking at least three times within the space of a few years; in September 2008, in May 2010, and in November 2011. In all three instances, the political motives behind the existence of the eurozone have proven stronger than the weaknesses of the vessel and the ineptness of its command. However, if this process continues for a while longer, it might not make much sense to have a common currency in Europe.

In today's world where artificially lowered interest rates are undermining the value of currencies, and policymakers are running out of ideas to kick-start weak economies, this report presents the Austrian Business Cycle Theory (ABCT) as an alternative to the mainstream economic line of thinking. The Austrian approach puts strong emphasis on innovation and entrepreneurship for the sustainability of a healthy economy, and promotes sound money policies. The hypothesis of our report is that if monetary expansion continues, then the euro will be unsustainable, and Germany should revert to the Deutschmark.

The structure of this thesis is as follows: we begin with a brief history of the Austrian School of economics, which discusses the emergence of the Austrian methodology, Austrian view regarding 'mainstream' thought, and identify predominant contributors to the Austrian School. This is followed by a detailed analysis of the Austrian Business Cycle Theory. The next chapter provides us with a theoretical look at the role that central banks play in the creation of a financial crisis. Having discussed this in great detail, we then highlight the fragility of the euro and how it may prove to be unsustainable in the future. The thesis also comprises of a chapter for evaluating the possibility of Germany reverting to the Deutschmark in response to current monetary instabilities. In addition, an elaborate discussion will be undertaken with particular emphasis on savings, money supply, interest rates, government debt and deficits, unemployment, inflation as well as deflation. Finally, a way forward is presented as recommendation in chapter 6, before the conclusion is drawn.

Unfortunately, the story of the European sovereign debt crisis had much more to do with politics, human behavior and an ever-expanding money supply than with predictable statistical models. So, analysis based on huge amounts of data crunching and risk models have proven to be insufficient and in certain cases led to entirely misleading predictions. That is why we believe that it is important for us to select deductive reasoning as the research methodology, instead of statistical models. Taking Austrian Business Cycle Theory as the starting point, we will use the following method to identify and observe the problems before deriving the right conclusion:

Figure 1 | Deductive Reasoning

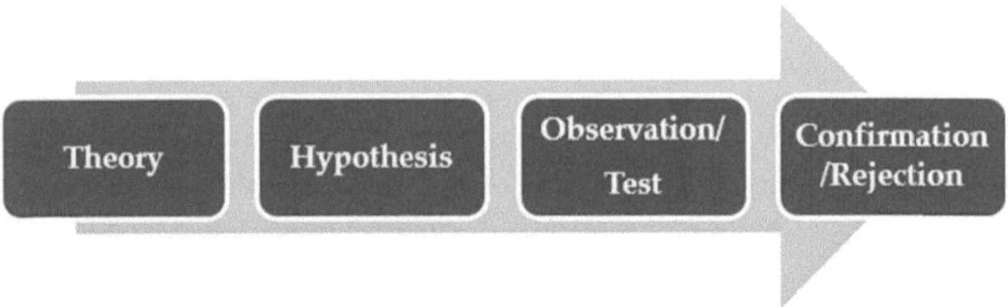

Now, understanding the causes of the sovereign debt crisis is vital if we want to overcome it. Bastasin (2012) identified two main interpretations of how the crisis evolved. They both begin with the observation that once the euro came into existence as a common currency, there was a significant reduction in real interest rates in the so-called peripheral countries within the European Monetary Union (EMU). These countries include Portugal, Ireland, Italy, Greece, and Spain (the acronym PIIGS is often used to denote these nations). According to the first analysis, German and French banks, among many other financial investors, were tempted to invest hundreds of billions of euros in the peripheral countries due to the absence of devaluation risks in the euro area. Within a short span of time, there was rapid movement of capital from the core countries to the periphery and this massive inflow of capital led to a sudden increase in domestic demand (both private and public consumption), in countries like Greece and Spain. These countries quickly became reliant on such foreign capital inflows, and people started living beyond their means, particularly in Greece. However, once the financial disruptions of 2008 culminated in a global crisis, the money started to dry up considerably due to increased risk aversion, and the external deficit in the peripheral countries thus became unsustainable.

The second analysis states that as a result of lower interest rates, the pressure on government debt service declined in the periphery, and government spending increased. Real estate bubbles started to develop in Ireland and Spain, and until 2007, revenue generated from these bubbles largely offset the significant increases in public spending. However, when financial conditions worsened and the bubbles burst, the precariousness of fiscal positions in the periphery came to the surface. So overall, low interest rates, reckless investments by German and French banks, fiscal profligacy, government indebtedness and low efficiency in the peripheral countries, all played a part in causing the sovereign debt crisis.

At the heart of this problem lies government intervention in the market. By buying government securities and artificially lowering interest rates, a central bank can trigger an increase in money supply and in the available funds for banks. The idea that governments could smooth out the volatility of free markets by expanding the supply of money and running large budget deficits in times of crisis is the main viewpoint of what is known as Keynesian economics. The theories forming the core of Keynesian economics were first presented by the British economist, John Maynard Keynes during the Great Depression of the 1930s. Keynesianism allows governments to pretend that they have the power to raise living standards with the assistance of a money printing press. The advocates of Keynes, called Keynesians, came into conflict with the "Austrian School" of economic thought which followed the views of economists like Ludwig von Mises and Frederick Hayek.

The Austrian economists have the opinion that recessions are necessary to compensate for unwise decisions made during the boom phase that always precede the bust in a business cycle. Austrians also believe that the booms are created by the false signals given to businessmen when governments artificially lower interest rates in the hope of stimulating economies. So, whereas the Keynesians look to mitigate the adverse impact of the busts, Austrians look to prevent artificial booms from happening in the first place.

In this report, we encapsulate under the name of Keynesianism, not only John Maynard Keynes's economic theories, but also the ideas of all schools of economic thought that seek to allow excessive government interventions. In our view, any government influence that extends far beyond the essential sovereign tasks of ensuring security and property rights should be considered excessive. So, just like Vogt & Leuschel (2011), we draw no distinction among multiple schools of economic thought, all of which demand a vigorous role for the government in the society and economy.

Woods (2009) notes the fact that the Austrians warned of the formation of bubbles and predicted the financial crash before anyone else did. Austrian economists consider the central bank to be the main culprit of financial crises. The Austrian approach to understanding what has happened to the economies of the world holds far greater explanatory power than does any competing school of thought. According to Hammond (2012), the most important contribution of the Austrian school to the field of economics is its theory of the business cycle (ABCT), which offers a unique, comprehensive and coherent description of the process of booms and busts that takes place frequently in a cyclical pattern. It highlights monetary intervention by the government in cooperation with the banking system as the origin of these booms and busts. So, let us now move on to the next chapter to discuss the Austrian school and its business cycle theory in greater detail.

Chapter 2: The Austrian School of Economic Thought

The Austrian School of economics is one of the oldest schools of economic thought. Birner & van Zijp (1994) highlights the fact that the Austrian School has contributed several major ideas to what can be termed 'mainstream' economics, most notably, the concepts of opportunity cost and subjective value. The Austrian School was founded by Carl Menger with the publication of *Grundsätze der Volkswirtschaftslehre* or *Principles of Economics* in 1871. The Austrian method is largely based on theoretical deductive reasoning based upon axioms of human action. By studying human action and reasoning logically, such seemingly complex economic phenomena as interest, prices, profits and inflation could be explained and understood as being grounded in the actions of individuals. They also strive to solve complex economic issues by means of outside-the-box thinking. Austrian economists believe that human behavior is too distinctive to be accurately modeled in mathematical terms and that it is best to have minimal government intervention in an economy.

The Austrian School places special emphasis on interest rates and according to them, it is determined by the time preference of borrowers and lenders. In other words, subjective decision of individuals to spend money now or in future determines the rate of interest. From an Austrian economist's point of view, business cycles are caused by distortion in interest rates due to the government's attempt to control money. When a government indulges in artificial manipulation of interest rates, it results in the misallocation of capital and resources.

Moreover, the Austrian School insists that innovation and entrepreneurial profit seeking are the two most important attributes that drives growth (Kirzner, 1997). According to them, entrepreneurship is central to creating the growth and prosperity that most Keynesian economists believe can be regulated by government intervention. Entrepreneurs are risk-takers, who combine labor and natural resources with the purpose of creating profit. The personal gain from the profit seeking activity helps not only the entrepreneur himself, but also raises the living standards of everyone else. Furthermore, entrepreneurs help to enhance productivity by utilizing resources efficiently, which makes it possible for people to consume more. So the economy does not actually prosper due to a rise in consumption first, but rather the increase in consumption is brought about as a result of the growth of an economy (Schiff & Schiff, 2010).

Austrian economists suggest that government intervention kills the entrepreneurial spirit by setting up regulatory obstacles to enter the markets, and high taxation also decreases the incentive to strive for success. However, if entrepreneurs do fail, the Austrian School is adamant about allowing them to be eliminated. Companies that are not able to survive are considered to be a misallocation of capital. Regardless of the size of these companies, those who have made wrong decisions must be discarded from the market and the capital which is left behind would then be reallocated and put to productive use. When such companies are bailed out by government money, the unprofitable companies are kept in business, which prevents the tied up capital from being better utilized elsewhere. Bailouts promote an environment of bad decision making, and the issue of moral hazard arises. Woods (2009) defines moral hazard as the increased likelihood of risky behavior arising whenever the acting party believes that any costs of his behavior will be borne not by himself alone but by a large group of people.

2.1 Money

Almost everybody wants more money, and we generally use money without thinking too much about its function. Few people are concerned about who controls the supply of money, where it comes from, or why it has value. Since money is an integral part of our daily lives, it is high time we take an interest in the aforementioned aspects to make sure that money remains sound and does not become something that keeps on losing value.

Due to the inconvenience of bartering (where goods are directly exchanged for other goods), money was invented out of necessity, and it has some major functions. Firstly, it is a medium of exchange, which has eliminated the inefficiencies of the barter system, by being generally accepted as payment for goods and services. Secondly, it is a unit of account which facilitates the calculation of valuation, and most importantly, price comparison. In addition, money is portable, implying convenience of usage, and last but not least, it is also supposed to act as a store of value.

For money to be valuable, it must have limited supply. Ever since 1971, when U.S. president Richard Nixon formally ended the convertibility of US dollars ($) to gold, all currencies have become fiat currencies (money not backed by anything). Fiat currency is considered as money solely because a sovereign government says it is money. It has no intrinsic metallic or redemption value, and its nominal value is what the government engraves on the face of the respective paper note or coin. However, the real value of fiat money is what it is worth in exchange for the currency of another country (Schiff & Downes, 2009). Bonner & Wiggin (2003) identifies clearly the main problem with all fiat currencies. It is that the fiat money managers may create more of it, as per their convenience, without giving due importance to the fact that they should never create so much that the illusion of scarcity is destroyed.

2.2 Business Cycles

A business cycle can be defined as fluctuations of aggregate economic activity. The most widely used measure of this is the gross domestic product (GDP) variable. Other measures that are included for a broader perspective on aggregate economic activity are unemployment figures and financial market figures, such as the short term interest rate. The Austrian School and Keynesians view business cycles in a contrasting manner. An Austrian business cycle goes from a period of expansion to a period of contraction and is measured from trough to trough, while in the eyes of Keynesians, an entire business cycle is a period of contraction followed by a period of expansion and is measured from peak to peak. The period of time where aggregate economic activity is growing is called the expansion or the boom phase. This phase goes from trough to peak. In contrast, a contraction or recession goes from peak to trough, and represents the period of time where aggregate economic activity is falling. If a recession is severe enough, it is referred to as a depression.

Austrians explain business cycles with particular focus placed on the money supply. They consider money supply, controlled largely by the central bank, to be explanatory of fluctuations in aggregate economic activity. Austrians are convinced that they know what causes the bubbles preceding a recession, while Keynesians believe that they have the necessary tools for avoiding a recession when it emerges. Therefore, it comes as no surprise that these two schools of economic thought always clash with each other due to the difference in viewpoints.

2.3 The Austrian Business Cycle Theory

The Austrian business cycle theory (abbreviated as ABCT) was first introduced by Ludwig von Mises in 1912 in the book "*The Theory of Money and Credit*" and has since been developed further. Two other predominant contributors to this development are Nobel Prize winner, Friedrich Hayek, and Murray Rothbard (Ebeling, 1978). ABCT focuses primarily on credit expansion, un-backed by savings, as being the cause of an unsustainable boom. Un-backed credit expansion results from interest rates prevailing in the economy at a rate much lower than that which clears the market. As interest rates coordinate present and future consumption, this un-backed credit expansion initiates a boom by distorting the productive structure of an economy with both unsound investments, mainly in interest sensitive producer goods, and overconsumption. This unsustainable boom is inevitably followed by a bust.

When the mistakes are exposed, the malinvestments, as Mises called them, are liquidated, creating the bust. Expansions that are financed by actual savings do not need such economic busts. It is only the un-backed credit expansion that sows the seeds of their ultimate demise. As Mises saw it, investors were not carelessly overinvesting; rather they were duped into responding to false economic signals sent to them courtesy of the easy money policy (excessive monetary expansion). According to Schiff & Downes (2009), this is the reason why Mises called such mistakes, malinvestments, instead of over-investments. In any case, these malinvestments must be liquidated, as prolonging their existence prevents the economy from shifting production and consumption patterns to those that would otherwise contribute to long-term growth. (Bagus & Howden, 2011)

Now, let us discuss in further detail, how credit expansion misdirects spending and investment in an economy. First of all, credit expansion implies an increase in the money supply but not an increase in real savings. Printing more money, or increasing the supply of credit, does not make more resources available. Such a monetary expansion causes interest rates to fall down even though there is no increase in real savings. At these artificially low rates, investment projects become profitable that would be unprofitable if the rates were higher. As we know, investment projects can be of varying lengths, so the entrepreneurs must decide which projects to start. A high interest rate would naturally make entrepreneurs more cautious and prevent them from tying up resources in long-term projects, unless they are sure that they can generate large gains from such investments. In contrast, a low interest rate reduces the risk associated with longer investments, and thus acts as a signal to tie capital up in lengthy projects (Murphy, 2016). As a result, investment projects are undertaken that cannot be successfully completed with the available real savings in the economy.

The second point to note regarding credit expansion is that it leads to an increased level of consumption, beyond what it would have been if interest rates had been at their natural (higher) rate. Just like in the case of any other good, the supply and demand of loanable funds goes up and down, and they determine the price (interest rate). In a free market economy, interest rates naturally go down if families are saving more or more banks are lending. By contrast, if there is a shortage of loanable funds, interest rates go up, making it costlier for investors to borrow money (Woods, 2009). In the absence of free market forces and enticed by the artificially reduced interest rate, people increase their current consumption, which naturally means that savings decline.

Third, there is a shift to the financial sector where credit expansion creates the greatest profits. Banks make use of this fresh liquidity prior to its use by others, thereby generating profits before Cantillon effects set in (see page 24-25 for details). Prices will rise only after other firms utilize the money. Moreover, Bagus & Howden (2011) explains that by extending loans against its deposit base, the financial sector creates new money endogenously, and attracts resources (and gains the associated profits) from all over the economy. Provided this process continues long enough, the banks ultimately find themselves in a situation where they are being surpassed (in relative profit terms) by firms engaging solely in financial speculation. It no longer remains beneficial for these institutions to earn money exclusively by relying on extending loans, instead speculation becomes the real profit driver, with profits relying on the continual influx of money and credit.[1]

According to the Austrian School, monetary expansion to finance government spending sows the seed for a business cycle to take place. This credit expansion not only causes significant increases in the money supply, but also large gains in asset prices (particularly in the housing and stock markets). As observed by the ABCT, artificially inflated prices during the boom period result in the eventual sharp decline in the value of stocks and housing. As the bust phase of the business cycle is a period where resources are reallocated to their highest value use, any policy which prevents this spontaneous market process from occurring, such as propping up of bankrupt firms, must be avoided. An important observation garnered from the Austrian Business Cycle Theory is that the economy will reallocate resources quicker in the absence of monetary intervention, resulting in a shorter recessionary period.

2.4 Credit Creation and Liquidation

In an ideal world, credit creation should be the result of savings by depositors in banks. In such a scenario, banks act as financial intermediaries and provide a link between savings and investment. People deposit money with the banks in return for interest and these savings are then loaned out to borrowers who also pay interest. The difference between the two rates of interest generates the profit for banks. However, what we witness nowadays is that most credit comes about through money printing which allows banks to issue loans that are not backed by adequate amount of savings. This type of credit expansion is a clear violation of the monetary irregular deposit contract. In this case, a bank's main purpose is to provide safety over the customer's assets. The bank is obliged to pay the full amount of the deposit if and when it is demanded by the customer. When this rule is not adhered to and money is printed out of thin air, the false signal entrepreneurs receive from this increased supply of credit is that there has been a rise in savings that will inevitably result in an increase in future consumption. This illusion brings about

[1] Philipp Bagus ("Asset Prices—An Austrian Perspective," Procesos de Mercado: Revista Europea de Economía Política 4, no. 2 [2007]: pp. 57–93, "Monetary Policy as Bad Medicine") discusses the herd behavior that results from this process.

an increase in the level of investments, which would not have taken place otherwise. (De Soto, 2009).

When the interest rate is set by genuine market forces, it gives the correct guidance to entrepreneurs and hence only the most profitable projects would be undertaken, without any malinvestments. If consumers are willing to defer immediate gratification, they save large amounts of their income, which frees up real resources from current consumption. Naturally, this pushes down interest rates and thus provides the right incentives for entrepreneurs to invest. In stark contrast, artificially lowering rates result in unnecessary investments and encourages the formation of unsustainable economic booms. F.A.Hayek was awarded the Nobel Prize in economics for explaining this phenomenon by showing how central bank manipulation of interest rates and money, create distortions throughout the economy and sets up the stage for an inevitable bust.

It must be said that in the beginning, the unsustainable expansion appears prosperous. Growth is visible in most industries, unemployment declines, while wages and commodity prices go up. However, sooner rather than later, it all comes crashing down. Woods (2009) points out that soon the realization strikes a large number of entrepreneurs that the pool of real savings is actually smaller than what they had initially anticipated. Thus the complementary factors of production turn out to be scarcer. The prices for labor and other resources will therefore be higher than expected, and business costs will rise. Firms will then need to borrow more to finance these unanticipated increases in input prices. This increased demand for loanable funds will raise the interest rate, thereby bringing into question the feasibility of some of these projects. To add to the woes, the banking sector starts to get nervous at this point. As banks become more reluctant to lend, interest rates start to rise even further. The tightening in the credit markets gradually becomes a source of pain for more and more businesses, especially the most leveraged ones. Entrepreneurs finally figure out that they were too ambitious, as it becomes impossible for them to complete the long-term projects they had begun. Workers get laid off as investment projects are abandoned, paving the way for the painful bust to set in.

Central banks often try to delay this painful period of financial reckoning, where the malinvestments are liquidated for an economy to be restored to its true health. They do this by cutting interest rates again and again. It is just like kicking a can down the road, hoping against hope that the inevitable would not happen, and the can will keep on rolling forever. Unfortunately, what they fail to realize is that the can will ultimately reach a dead-end. They do this in order to maintain labor employment by keeping unhealthy businesses afloat, but this only prolongs and enlarges the adverse effects of the credit injection. As a consequence, the corrections in the market become much larger in magnitude, making the subsequent recession significantly worse.

Instead of letting the markets function under the pricing mechanism, Keynes believed that government spending and monetary injection into the economy could instigate a rise in demand for the goods of companies, and keep people employed. The key point here is that Keynesians want to prevent the bust, whereas Austrians want to prevent the artificial booms, created by false signals in the markets (Schiff & Schiff, 2010). Moreover, as mentioned earlier, Austrians argue that unprofitable companies should be allowed to fail and go out of business. This would open up the possibility for entrepreneurs with excess capital to purchase the valuable assets for profit seeking activities. Such a process would assist in creating new sustainable businesses and related employment.

Writing during the Great Depression of the 1930s, F.A. Hayek highlighted the adverse effect of an easy money policy:

> *To combat the depression by a forced credit expansion is to attempt to cure the evil by the very means which brought it about; because we are suffering from a misdirection of production, we want to create further misdirection – a procedure that can only lead to a much more severe crisis as soon as the credit expansion comes to an end.*[2]

Robbins (1934) reiterates that nobody likes unemployment and bankruptcy, but they would not have been necessary had the artificial boom not been stimulated in the first place. Producer-goods industries attract more investment than the consumer-goods industries because

---

[2] See F. A. Hayek, *Prices and Production and Other Works*, ed. Joseph T. Salerno (Auburn, Ala.: Ludwig von Mises Institute)

that sector is the most sensitive to interest-rate changes, and so the impact of the downturn is felt heavier there. In a similar vein, Ron Paul (2009) continues by stating that when the need arises, liquidation is necessary and will eventually prove to be beneficial. The financial world requires this form of liquidation now.

2.5 Criticisms of ABCT

As with any other theory, over the years, some criticisms regarding ABCT have been raised by economists belonging to different schools of thought. This discussion will mention the two main critiques of ABCT, and refute them along the way.

First of all, based on the rational expectations hypothesis (REH), developed by American economist Muth (1961), several economists have criticized ABCT arguing that the theory requires economic agents to display a certain degree of economic irrationality. Caplin (1997) raises an important question: why are entrepreneurs tricked into excessive investing by government-induced artificial low interest rates, instead of correctly predicting central bank policy and realizing that interest rates will be higher in the future? To refute this, Callahan (2006) asks a counter-question: considering the fact that central banks throughout the world has been manipulating interest rates for a protracted period of time, how would an entrepreneur actually determine the 'natural' rate of interest in the first place? For businessmen to figure out the distortionary effects of un-backed credit expansion, widespread knowledge of ABCT would be necessary, which is unfortunately not the case today (Davidson, 2013). Even those entrepreneurs, who have a clear understanding of the Austrian theory, may still find it hard to resist the temptation of borrowing money when interest rates are artificially low. They may consider it to be advantageous to invest while rates are low and attempt to ride the boom. A new project might be launched in the hope that it will be one of the lucky ones and that the entrepreneur will be able to get out before the downturn hits. Woods (2009) suggests that if these businessmen are clever enough not to react to the artificially lowered rates, their competitors surely will, which might enable them to gain market share at the former's expense. So, it becomes part of human nature to take the bait.

Tulloch (1988) points out another criticism of ABCT, which is that the theory does not explain why inflation cannot be continued indefinitely. In response, Rothbard (2009) states that continued inflationary policies will be met with a decreased demand for cash holdings by the general public. Cash holdings will decrease as there will be increased investment in goods which might eventually instigate a period of hyperinflation and a flight from the currency. Let us now move on to the next segment for a more detailed discussion about the important concept of inflation.

2.6 Inflation

The Austrian School has the firm opinion that any increase in money supply which is not accommodated by a rise in the production of goods and services leads to an increase in prices. However, the prices of all goods do not increase simultaneously. Prices of some goods may increase comparatively faster, while the first users of the newly printed money benefit at the expense of others, leading to greater disparities in the economy.

A central bank is supposed to be independent, but to a large extent, it actually ends up complying with the policies of the government in the financial markets. This means that it tries to eliminate business cycles by printing money and financing deficit spending to avoid recessions. When the central bank injects money into the financial system, the private banks expand their level of credit. In this way, the Austrian School sees inflation as an increase in the money supply which causes prices to rise, thereby posing a big danger to society (Schiff & Downes, 2009). Most politicians and economists insist on defining inflation as a rising price level, when in fact, rising prices is a harmful consequence of monetary inflation. While attending a conference on the Economics of Mobilization, held at West Virginia, in April 1951, Ludwig von Mises elaborated on the definition of inflation by stating that:

> *People today use the term "inflation" to refer to the phenomenon that is an inevitable consequence of inflation, that is the tendency of all prices and wage rates to rise. The result of this deplorable confusion is that there is no term left to signify the cause of this rise in prices and wages....Those who pretend to fight inflation are in fact only fighting what is the inevitable consequence of inflation, rising prices. Their ventures are doomed to failure because they do not*

attack the root of the evil. They try to keep prices low while firmly committed to a policy of increasing the quantity of money that must necessarily make them soar. [3]

So in simple words, contrary to the generally accepted view, inflation is not a general rise in prices, but rather it is a term that denotes an increase in the money stock. Mises claimed that this confusion over defining inflation was mischievous and a deliberate attempt by governments to get people to focus only on prices when thinking about inflation. Paul (2008) suggests that if we understood inflation properly as an increase in money supply, we would instantly know that the best way to cure it is by placing a demand on the central banks to cease manipulating the money stock. Moreover, Paul (2009) adds that if it is considered only as a price problem, then blame can be attached to speculators and profiteers. This deflects attention away from the real source of the problem which is the central bank and its money printing press. Hence, the central bank's role in the inflation is largely ignored.

Austrians believe that a rise in the money supply do not always manifest in economy-wide increases in the consumer price index, which is considered as the standard definition of inflation. Instead, the excess cash might flow into specific areas of the economy, depending on real-world factors (Doherty, 2012). According to Paul (2008), it is also wrong to believe that prices rise in conjunction with wages and salaries, and as a result, inflation causes no real problems. In order to explain how inflation benefits certain parties at the expense of others, he highlighted the distribution effects, or Cantillon effects of inflation, (named after economist Richard Cantillon):

> *The price increases that take place as a result of inflation do not occur all at once and to the same degree. Those who receive the new money first receive it before prices have yet risen. They enjoy a windfall. Meanwhile, as they spend the new money, and the next wave of recipients spend it, and so on, prices begin to rise throughout the economy – well before the new money has trickled down to most people. The average person is now paying higher prices while still earning his old income, which has not yet been adjusted to account for the higher money supply....The enrichment of the politically well connected – in other words, those who get the*

[3] As quoted in *The Commercial and Financial Chronicle, April 26, 1951.*

newly created money first: government contractors, big banks, and the like – comes at the direct expense of everyone else.[4]

To sum it up, expansionary monetary policies create inflation. Stabilizing prices is a priority for both the Austrians and Keynesians, but the tools they use are totally different. In the mainstream Keynesian line of thinking, the economy needs stimulus to avoid recessions, which for Austrian economists is equivalent to the creation of widespread inflation.

2.7 Deflation

Deflation is commonly defined as a fall in the price level. The real definition of deflation would be a decline in the supply of money. So, it the opposite of inflation, and is another form of saying that money becomes more valuable over time. Deflation can be economically clarifying as it causes banks to tighten up their lending standards and encourages businesses to run tighter operations. Deflation also raises the real value of government debt and it can actually act as a restraint on government spending, as it becomes harder to service the debt.

It is true that deflation can become a major cause for concern when demand disappears due to a complete collapse of income in an economy. However, that is an extreme case as generally, there is always demand at some level of prices. In simple terms, deflation means that supply exceeds demand, causing consumer prices to fall. According to Schiff & Downes (2009), most economists worry about falling prices for two main reasons. The first concern is that people will stop spending and postpone purchases, as they anticipate cheaper prices, but there is no evidence to justify the notion that this actually happens. He dismissed this concern by pointing out that computers and cell phones are becoming cheaper day by day, but they continue to sell in large volumes.

The other fear is that corporate profits would take a hit, causing companies to reduce production, downsize and reduce future investments. However, what most people tend to forget is that profitability is about margins. When costs and prices fall together, margins remain the

[4] See Ron Paul, 2008 p. 103

same. In fact, constant margins often lead to greater profitability, as sales increase due to falling prices.

Neo-classical Keynesian theory has generated deflation paranoia, and created an almost universal acceptance that prices must keep on increasing to prevent a fall in prices. It must be said that falling prices is not always good for an economy, but there is also a good form of deflation, which Keynesians tend to ignore. Austrians argue that some prices fall naturally over time due to competition, efficiency, innovation and technological progress. Computers, mobile phones and televisions can be considered as prime examples of technological goods that have become both better and cheaper, over the years.

2.8 Summary

Having discussed inflation and deflation at length, let us now recap some of the other important issues that we have covered in this chapter:

- Economists belonging to the Austrian School believe that human behavior cannot be accurately modeled in mathematical terms and puts emphasis on the distortion in interest rates brought about by the government's attempt to control money to explain why we experience frequent booms and busts.
- It is a common fallacy of the Keynesians that increasing consumption can be the solution to current economic problems. In reality, an economy does not prosper due to a rise in consumption first, but rather the increase in consumption is brought about by the growth of the economy.
- The Austrian Business Cycle Theory (ABCT) highlights that interest rates can come down in two ways: either naturally when the general population saves more; or artificially when central banks force the rate down.
- If interest rates are lowered, businessmen respond by starting new projects. These projects are usually undertaken in the most interest-rate sensitive areas, especially in the so-called higher-order stages of production: construction, raw materials, and capital equipments to name a few. In other words, these are the production processes that are farthest removed in time from finished consumer goods.

- When the interest rate is lower because of a natural cause like increased saving, then the market works efficiently without any hiccups. The decision of the general public to defer consumption to a later date provides the incentive and necessary resources for the new investment projects initiated by businesses' to be seen through to completion. However, if the interest rate is lower because of artificial manipulation by a central bank then the aforementioned projects cannot all be completed. The essential materials needed to complete them have not been saved by the public, and hence it is soon discovered that investors have been duped into production lines that cannot be sustained.
- Once these malinvestments become apparent, ABCT suggests that it is essential to liquidate them. The sooner the monetary manipulation comes to an end, the faster malinvestments can be eradicated and misallocated resources are redirected into sustainable ventures. On the other hand, the longer governments try to prop things up in the form of bailouts and rescue packages, the worse the inevitable bust will become in the future.

Chapter 3: Central Banks and Monetary Union

Now, let us discuss in detail, the major roles of a central bank. The mission of a central bank is to provide the nation with a safe and stable financial system. Its main functions are: (i) being the bank of the government and commercial banks, (ii) being the lender of last resort, and (iii) regulating the banking system and managing monetary policies (Parkin et al., 1997).

Being the bank of the government means financing its spending which can be done in two ways. It can be done either by issuing a direct loan which is equivalent to money printing, or alternatively, by selling government bonds. The central bank changes the supply of money by buying or selling bonds in the bonds market in what is called open market operations. If it wants to decrease the amount of money in circulation it sells existing bonds in the market, thereby removing money from the existing supply. On the other hand, if the central bank wishes to increase the amount of money in the economy, it buys bonds by creating money (Blanchard, 2003). The price of these bonds and their interest rates has an inverse relationship. The lower the bond price, the higher the interest rate and vice versa. Thus, financing debt through open market operations can be used to control the interest rate in financial markets.

Being the bank of the commercial banks imply keeping their reserves, regulating the banking sector and acting as their lender of last resort. When central banks extend credit to commercial banks in times of a credit crunch, it means they are serving the purpose of being a lender of last resort. Restoring the cash levels of commercial banks helps to avoid a possible bank run. In theory, the central bank can also regulate the money supply by increasing the minimum reserve requirement.

A central bank can also directly set the interest rate at which commercial banks borrow funds. Increasing the interest rate makes it more costly to loan money from the central bank, encouraging commercial banks to cut down on their lending, while a fall in the interest rate naturally stimulates lending. The banks are required to keep a specific fraction of their deposits on reserve, to be made available for customer withdrawal. Banks can find themselves below the reserve requirement set by the central bank if they have made a lot of loans or if an unusually large number of people have withdrawn funds. Banks borrow from each other when the need arises for additional cash reserves to meet this reserve requirement. The interest rate increases when there is too much demand from banks looking to borrow and too little supply from banks willing to lend. A central bank, like the Federal Reserve of the United States, then intervenes by buying bonds from the banks. This gives the banks more money in the form of reserves to lend to banks that need it. In the process, funds available to be lent to other banks become more abundant, and a correspondingly lower interest rate reflects this. So, a question may now arise regarding from where exactly a central bank can get hold of this money to buy the bonds. Paul (2008) provided a simple answer to this query by stating that the central bank creates the money out of thin air by writing checks on itself and then giving them to the banks.

3.1 The European Central Bank (ECB)

The European Central Bank (ECB) is at the heart of European monetary union. The ECB was envisioned in the Maastricht Treaty (1992) and legally formed in 1998. It is responsible for issuing the euro, which is a single currency for nineteen out of the twenty eight nations that are European Union (EU) members. Moreover, the ECB conducts monetary policy with the mandate of maintaining price stability in the eurozone. It also manages the foreign exchange reserves of the nineteen national central banks in the eurozone (countries using the euro) and operates a payments platform among those banks called TARGET2.

The European System of Central Banks (ESCB) consists of the European Central Bank (ECB) and the national central banks of the EU member states. The ESCB is governed by the decision-making bodies of the ECB, which consists of the Governing Council and the Executive Board (ECB, 2002). The Governing Council (comprising nineteen national governors) of the ECB is empowered to formulate monetary policy, while the Executive Board of six members is responsible for implementing the monetary policy according to the guidelines established and decisions made by the Governing Council. If its multinational nature is taken into consideration, the ECB is definitely quite distinct from all other central banks. It is responsible for shaping the combined monetary policy in a system consisting of nineteen countries, each of which retains considerable control of the other relevant economic policy instruments.

3.2 Money Creation by the ECB

Now, let us take a look at how the ECB can use monetary operations to indulge in money creation. To start off, when governments wish to spend more than they receive in taxes, they issue bonds. The ECB is not supposed to buy these bonds outright. However, this changed with the recent sovereign debt crisis, as will be discussed in detail later.

Banks will buy such a bond from the government, possibly by creating new money, because they know that it can be used as collateral. The ECB then accepts the bond (as collateral) in a reverse transaction, thereby lending money to the banks. A reverse transaction is an operation whereby the central bank conducts credit operations against collateral or buys/sells assets under a repurchase agreement (repo). Once the maturity date is reached (usually one week or a month), the ECB simply renews the loan and keeps the bond as collateral, if it wants to maintain the money supply. The ECB can continue to do this for as long as ten years. After this time period expires, the government will have to pay back the bond and normally does so by issuing another bond. Hence, the process goes on in this manner. In other words, the government never has to pay its debt; rather it simply issues new debt to pay for the old one. Moreover, from the interest payment that is paid to the ECB, a part of it actually flows back to the government, as ECB profits are remitted according to the capital of the different national central banks.

The ECB uses three main instruments for its monetary policy: (i) open market operations (ii) standing facilities and (iii) changes in minimum reserves.

According to Bagus (2010), there are basically two main ways to create money via open market operations. The first option enables a central bank to purchase or sell securities outright. As discussed earlier, this is how the Federal Reserve (Fed) of the USA prefers to carry out its open market operations. However, outright purchase or sale of securities is not officially a viable option for the ECB, when it comes to manipulating the money supply, and so it uses the other method by lending new money to banks through its lending facilities. This consists of the structural refinancing facility, the fine tuning facility, the long term refinancing facility and the main refinancing facility. In these facilities, securities are not purchased but used in reversed transactions: repos or collateralized loans.

In a repo, the ECB gets hold of a security with new money and sells it back at a higher price (difference is the amount of interest). A collateralized loan is similar to a repo with the only difference being the issue of legal ownership. In the case of a collateralized loan, ownership of the bond stays with the bank that pledged it as collateral, while in a repo, the ownership of the collateral changes to the ECB.

The ECB has always accepted a broader range of collateral compared to other central banks like the Fed of the USA, thus in essence, making its policies comparatively more flexible. The Fed only accepts or buys AAA rated securities in its open market operations.[5] In contrast, alongside government bonds, the ECB also accepts mortgage backed securities, and other debt instruments that are at least rated A−. As an emergency measure, this minimum rating was reduced to BBB− during the sovereign debt crisis because of the poor ratings of Greek bonds. Eventually, the situation became so bad that the decision was made to accept Greek bonds, regardless of their rating.

The difference between open market operations and standing facilities (the marginal lending facility and the deposit facility) is that the initiative of open market operations lies on the part of the ECB, whereas banks initiate standing facilities. Through the deposit facility, banks can receive interest by depositing money overnight at the ECB (Bagus, 2010). The rate of the deposit facility is the lower limit for interbank rates. No bank would accept a comparatively lower rate for funds in the interbank market because it can get the deposit facility rate at the ECB. On the other hand, in the marginal lending facility, banks can borrow money from the ECB at penalty rates and it represents the upper limit for the interbank rate.

Finally, expansion of credit is also possible by reducing the required minimum reserves that banks must hold in their accounts at the ECB. The opposite scenario of money being taken out of the economy happens in the case of an increase in minimum reserves. This instrument was

---

[5] *See Federal Reserve, "The Federal Reserve System: Purposes and Functions,"9th ed. (2005), http://www.federalreserve.gov, p. 39–40.) In the discount window, investment grade securities are accepted (rated BBB– and higher). (Ibid., p. 50.)*

generally not used and required reserves for demand deposits were held constant at two percent till the end of 2011. However, this rate has been reduced to one percent since 18 January 2012.

3.3 Differences between the Bundesbank and the ECB

Before the ECB came into existence, the government of France knew that giving assurance to the German government of ECB's independence from political interventions was necessary for the implementation of a monetary union. The French politicians actually always felt confident that if the necessity arose, the ECB could be used to serve political purposes. Marsh (1992) argues that the most important motive behind the campaign for European monetary union was France's desire to shackle the Bundesbank's monetary dominance, and bring about the demise of the Deutschmark (DM).

On the other hand, German politicians believed that the ECB would be like a copy of the prestigious Bundesbank, thereby assisting in bringing stability to the rest of Europe. Marsh (1992) further observes that Germany is one of the few countries in the world where central bank presidents know that tough monetary policies can actually help to enhance their reputation. Hence, preserving sound money and the overall reputation of the Bundesbank always used to take precedence over other matters, including allegiance to the Chancellor. Due to the fact that Germany's anti-inflation policy was a direct result of history, Dieter Hiss, the former president of the Berlin Landeszentralbank, questioned whether it would ever be possible to transfer this inflation-averse mindset outside German borders. He pointed out that Germany's need for stability is the result of a painful learning process from a time when savings were wiped out twice within a period of less than thirty years. This form of behavior based on first-hand experience is difficult to pass on to others around the world. Therefore, the key to this German mentality lies firmly rooted in the experience of hyper-inflation of the 1920s.

Needless to say, in the absence of monetary stability, prosperity can be neither created nor sustained. If we take into consideration the decade from 1980 to 1990, the Bundesbank managed to achieve its annual monetary target eight times and failed to meet the goal only three times in that time period, as depicted in the table below:

Table 1 | German Money Supply and Inflation Performance (1980 – 1990)

Year	Money Supply Target (%)	Actual Outcome	Target Met (Yes/ No)	Inflation Rate (%)
1980	5-8	5	Yes	5.5
1981	4-7	4	Yes	6.3
1982	4-7	6	Yes	5.2
1983	4-7	7	Yes	3.3
1984	4-6	5	Yes	2.4
1985	3-5	5	Yes	2.0
1986	3.5-5.5	8	No	-0.1
1987	3-6	8	No	0.2
1988	3-6	7	No	1.3
1989	5	5	Yes	2.8
1990	4-6	6	Yes	2.7

Source: Marsh, 1992

Marsh (1992) duly notes that the Bundesbank regards combating inflation as a form of art, where monetary technicalities are pushed to the background, while judgment is always prioritized. In the end, the Bundesbank and the ECB turned out to be quite different from each other in the ways they both operate. One major difference is in the accountability of the two institutions. The Bundesbank remained totally independent and managed German monetary policy directly. Politicians never really attempted to influence the Bundesbank because Germans are normally very inflation-averse and hence pursuing inflationary policies would have had adverse effects on the politicians. In contrast, nowadays, if there is price inflation in the eurozone, German politicians can blame others for the rise in prices by stating that they opposed inflationary monetary measures, but were simply outvoted by their European contemporaries.[6]

[6] See *Stefan Homburg, Hat die Waehrungsunion Auswirkungen auf die Finanzpolitik?," in Franz-Ulrich Willeke, ed., Die Zukunft der D-Mark. Eine Streitschrift zur Europaeischen Waerungsunion (Muenchen: Olzog, 1997), p. 93-108)*

The variance in the functions of the two institutions is another important issue. The main task of the Bundesbank is price stability. The role of the ECB is more ambitious. The Treaty of Maastricht states that its primary objective *"shall be to maintain price stability."* Yet, *"without prejudice of the objective of price stability, the Eurosystem shall support the general economic policies in the Community"* (Tommaso, 2004). This addition is the result of pressure from the French government, which had always wanted direct political control over money printing. Bagus (2012) reiterates that while the Bundesbank focused only on containing monetary stability, the ECB has a second pillar, which is to rely on economic indicators like wage rates, long term interest rates, exchange rates, output measures, price indexes etc. in its monetary policy decisions. Therefore, the ECB has more discretionary power compared to the Bundesbank.

3.4 The Maastricht Treaty

The Bundesbank was given the responsibility of drafting the statute of the ECB. Unsurprisingly, it put firm emphasis on a mandate for price stability and independence from political interference. Moreover, it was determined that the new central bank's ability to finance government budget deficits should be limited, just like in the case of the Bundesbank. Eichengreen (2011) notes that in order to participate in the monetary union, countries were obliged to bring down their inflation, budget deficits and debts. All these provisions went into the draft treaty agreed upon at the summit in the Dutch city of Maastricht.

The Maastricht Treaty was signed on 7 February 1992 by the members of the European Community, thereby establishing economic and monetary union (EMU) as a formal objective, ultimately leading to the creation of the euro. The treaty specified some convergence criteria, which clearly showed that Germany tried to establish its views on how a monetary union should be formed. First and foremost, it was affirmed that well-defined limits on budgetary and economic policies must be put in place, if outright political union is not considered to be a possibility. Admission into the monetary union was only made possible for those countries that fulfilled the following convergence criteria:

(i) An inflation rate not more than 1.5 percent higher than the average of the three lowest inflation rates among the candidate members.

(ii) A long-term interest rate not more than 2 percent higher than the average observed in the three countries with the lowest inflation rates.

(iii) A government budget deficit not higher than 3 percent of Gross Domestic Product (GDP). In exceptional circumstances, countries with higher budget deficit can be permitted to enter, provided the deficit is declining continuously and should remain close to 3 percent.

(iv) A government debt not exceeding 60 percent of GDP. If a country has higher level of government debt, it should diminish sufficiently and approach 60 percent at a satisfactory pace.

(v) Members should not experience devaluation during the two years preceding entrance into the union.

Two other stipulations of the Maastricht Treaty proved to be critical in subsequent years. First, national central banks or the ECB were not allowed to directly finance government budget deficits of any kind. Secondly, the treaty stipulated a no bailout clause, which implied that no individual member of the European Union could be held liable for the financial commitments of any other member.

On January 1, 1999, the EMU became reality, and the exchange rates of the currencies of the EMU member states were irreversibly locked, although initially, the euro existed only as a unit of account. Eventually, on January 1, 2002, the national currencies of the EMU members were replaced by euro notes and coins. The starting group consisted of Austria, Belgium, Finland, France, Germany, Ireland, Italy, Luxembourg, the Netherlands, Portugal, and Spain. Greece adopted the single currency in 2001, followed by Slovenia in 2007, Cyprus and Malta in 2008, Slovakia in 2009, and Estonia in 2011. Latvia joined in 2014, and the following year, Lithuania became the newest member of the euro club.

The German government had tried to impose automatic sanctions in the case of any infringement of the deficit limit, but in 1996, other governments rejected automatic sanctions on countries with deficit overruns. In fact, as per 2010 data, all but one member state had violated the three percent maximum limit on deficits. Moreover, the average European debt ratio to GDP stood at eighty-eight percent. At the time the Maastricht Treaty was signed, many countries that wanted to join the EMU did not meet the deficit and debt criteria. Overtveldt (2011) highlights the fact that Italy's budget deficit in 1993 stood at 10 percent of GDP, while Spain and France had 7 and 6 percent deficit, respectively. In the same year, Italy's government debt was 116 percent of GDP, far exceeding the limit of 60 percent. While several countries went for genuine policy initiatives to cut budget deficits, others decided to come up with ways to artificially lower it.

Monetary union was built on the assumption that fiscal rules, strictly applied, would be enough to ensure that countries play by the rules. However, things certainly did not turn out that way as Greece started fudging the rules courtesy of some fake accounting, even before it entered the eurozone in 2001, and never properly abided by the established limits. Unfortunately, France and Germany were also among the violators of the limits, alongside the peripheral countries. In fact, based on a yearly report published by the European Commission, before 2011, there were around seventy cases of violations of the 3 percent deficit threshold that could not possibly be justified by the economic downturn.[7] For instance, if we consider the year 2003, Germany, France, Portugal, Italy and Greece all exceeded the 3 percent limit (see Table 2). It must be said that things have improved somewhat in recent years with Italy and Ireland managing to bring the deficit below the threshold. However, currently (based on 2015 data) the situation is nowhere near good enough as countries like France, Portugal, Greece and Spain still has a deficit beyond the limit. If we look at the data for the two decades from 1995 to 2015, it can be clearly seen that Germany is the only country that managed to improve its position drastically from a deficit of 9.4% to a surplus of 0.7%. The other noteworthy improvement came in Italy, where the deficit has declined from 7.3% to a more manageable 2.6%.

[7] The European Commission publishes a yearly report: "European Economy – Public Finance in the EMU."

Table 2 | Government Deficit/Surplus in Germany, France and PIIGS (% of GDP)

Nation	1995	1999	2003	2007	2011	2015
Germany	-9.4	-1.7	-4.2	0.2	0.2	0.7
France	-5.1	-1.6	-3.9	-2.7	-2.5	-3.5
Portugal	-5.2	-3.0	-4.4	-3.0	-7.4	-4.4
Ireland	-2.1	2.4	0.4	0.3	-12.6	-2.3
Italy	-7.3	-1.8	-3.4	-1.5	-3.5	-2.6
Greece	-9.7	-5.8	-7.8	-6.7	-10.2	-7.2
Spain	-7.0	-1.3	-0.4	2.0	-9.6	-5.1

Source: Eurostat

When government debts are taken into consideration, the outlook is even more dismal. Since the commencement of the crisis, none of the PIIGs along with Germany and France have managed to bring the level down to anywhere near the 60% threshold. For most of the nations, debts just keep on piling up with no signs of declining. The fact that currently the debt levels of Portugal and Italy are more than twice the limit, and exceeds it by almost three times in Greece is simply astounding to comprehend. The severity of the problem is illustrated below:

Table 3 | Government Debt in Germany, France and PIIGS (% of GDP)

Nation	1999	2007	2011	2013	2015
Germany	61.3	65.2	81.7	77.2	71.2
France	59.0	64.2	85.4	92.4	95.8
Portugal	49.6	68.3	105.6	129	129
Ireland	48.5	24.8	106.6	120	93.8
Italy	113.7	103.1	120.9	129	132.7
Greece	100.3	107.4	161.7	177.7	176.9
Spain	62.4	36.2	69.6	93.7	99.2

Source: DB Global Markets Research, Eurostat, Haver Analytics

3.5 Pros and Cons of Monetary Union

Of course, there are quite a few advantages of forming a monetary union. For instance, in the case of a single currency, there are no exchange rate risks within the union. Devaluation is not possible with the single currency, so this reduces trade tensions and protectionist policy measures. The single currency can help to stimulate trade, enhance investment, reduce uncertainty, and overall, the absence of currency conversion costs contributes to economic efficiency.

According to Overtveldt (2011), another strong argument in favor of the EMU is that the single currency made member states less dependent on the wide fluctuations of the dollar, which is still the reserve currency of the world. The population and economic strength of the eurozone positioned the euro as an equal to the dollar in the international financial arena. Finally, the monetary union was also established for political reasons as European politicians were determined to avoid a repetition of the devastating world wars the European continent had to endure in the past.

However, problems crop up when it comes to quantifying the impact of these advantages. For instance, the prevention of war between member countries is certainly a great achievement, but the question arises as to how much credit, if any, can actually be attributed to the monetary union for preserving peace. Furthermore, the economic, political, and other benefits of monetary union are based on the assumption that the union functions smoothly and efficiently. Lower transaction costs, greater price transparency, stable exchange rates, and more integrated financial systems have little value without economic and financial stability. At the end of the day, the long-term viability of the monetary union depends on whether the union's institutional environment is strong enough to prevent large-scale financial instability. (Overtveldt, 2011)

A major disadvantage of joining the monetary union is the loss of an independent monetary policy. A union's common monetary policy may prove to be too tight for the economy of one member country and too loose for another. Significant deviations may lead to a rise in the level of unemployment, higher inflation, and swelling deficits. The monetary union should look to correct imbalances in the economies of member countries as soon as they materialize and the best approach would be to let market forces correct these imbalances.

The loss of the variable exchange rate as an economic policy tool is yet another disadvantage. When a country loses competitiveness because of increased internal costs in comparison with international costs, variable exchange rates give a country the option of devaluing its currency to regain competitiveness. Member countries of a currency union cannot use the option of devaluation and hence, can only pursue internal deflation, which is a nominal decline in labor and other internal costs. However, Overtveldt (2011) argues that this deflationary process is difficult to implement, especially in countries where powerful interest groups may offer fierce resistance.

3.6 Optimum Currency Area

The economic theory of optimum currency area (OCA) provides a list of the following eight conditions required for a smoothly functioning monetary union:

(i) Price and wage flexibility. Corden (1972) points out that such flexibility helps to prevent higher unemployment, inflation and cost disadvantages.

(ii) Similar inflation rates. When inflation rates between countries remain low and similar over time, there will also be fairly stable terms of trade between these countries, thus reducing the need for nominal exchange rate adjustments. Fleming (1971) observes that differences in inflation rates inevitably result in cost disadvantages for higher-inflation countries.

(iii) Mobility of labor and other factors of production. Mundell (1961) argues that the greater this mobility, the better the economic system will adjust to unexpected shocks, and the smaller the cost associated with the loss of an independent monetary policy.

(iv) Fiscal integration. Kenen (1969) highlights the need for monetary unions to have transparent fiscal transfer mechanisms to redistribute funds. This would enable them to adjust to economic shocks, as smoothly as possible. Fiscal integration also reduces the need for independent monetary policies and exchange rate adjustments.

(v) Political integration. Austrian economist Haberler (1970) stresses the importance of similar policy attitudes and convictions among member countries, which should ultimately lead to convergence in economic development.

(vi) Financial integration. According to Ingram (1962), when the financial markets of a union's member countries are well integrated, small differences in interest rates will bring about capital flows to cushion the adjustment to adverse disturbances. Financial integration can also help to reduce the need for exchange rate adjustments.

(vii) Degree of diversification of the individual economies. Specific sectors of countries with more diverse economies are less vulnerable to asymmetric shocks and will feel the effects of such shocks to a lesser degree. (Kenen, 1969)

(viii) Degree of openness of the individual economies. Mckinnon (1963) argues that the more open an economy, the less useful an exchange rate adjustment becomes for correcting asymmetric shocks or cost disadvantages.

Fulfillment of these eight elements will synchronize the business cycle throughout the monetary union and provided the cycle is well synchronized, the need for nation-specific macroeconomic policies will be reduced. However, the original eleven EMU member countries did not meet all of the OCA conditions. Overtveldt (2011) points out that flexibility of wages and prices, mobility of labor, fiscal integration, and political integration were only weakly met. The EMU was more successful in satisfying the conditions of similar inflation rates, financial integration, degree of diversification, and degree of openness.

David Archer, assistant governor of the Reserve Bank of New Zealand, put forward his views regarding the atmosphere surrounding the discussion on EMU and OCA criteria by stating that:

> *EMU had something to do with the theory of optimal currency areas. On the few occasions that I was present at pre-EMU conferences where the prospect of EMU was under discussion, only the Anglo-Saxon (mainly North American) economists present were approaching the issue from the perspective of optimal currency analysis. The European economists present either recognized the paramount place of political motivation, or focused on other facets of the economic analysis.*[8]

Now, the United States can definitely be considered as "the world's most successful single currency union."[9] It has a shared culture and a common language. In addition, based on the views expressed by Kim (1998) and Margo (1998), the United States had significant mobility of labor and capital long before it became a monetary union and its labor market is less rigid

[8] Archer as quoted in Artis, 2002, p. 23
[9] See Tilford, 2006, p. 11

compared to the EMU members. Labor mobility is up to three times higher in the United States than in Europe (OECD, 1999). As a study conducted in 2010 emphasized:

> *Despite the fact that there has been significant progress in the legal and political framework of the free movement of workers, as well as favourable opinion on free movement among the EU citizens, labor mobility is still very low... a number of legal, administrative, cultural and behavioural barriers [remain].*[10]

If, for instance, capital in the form of equipment and plant could shift from Germany to Portugal to take advantage of abundant labor, or if labor could shift from Portugal to Germany to take advantage of abundant capital, then it would be possible to solve the unemployment problem without resorting to inflation. EU directives and the use of the euro have helped significantly when it comes to increasing the mobility of capital, but unfortunately Europe has lagged behind in mobility-of-labor terms, mainly due to linguistic and cultural differences among the nations.

Besides that issue, the timing of bringing about a political and monetary union is also completely different, if one takes the experiences of the United States and Europe into account. In the United States of America, political union preceded monetary union by several decades. On the other hand, in Europe, monetary union was created as a means to political union, and not the other way around. The sad reality is that Europe is still nowhere close to attaining that political union.

So overall, it is fair enough to suggest that institutional adjustments must be made to bring the EMU significantly more in line with the prescriptions of the theory of optimum currency areas. Effective functioning of a monetary union depends on the fulfillment of these aforementioned conditions, and there is still plenty of scope for improvement in the EMU when it comes to fulfilling the conditions of labor mobility, price and wage flexibility, political union, and fiscal integration.

---

[10] See Smigiel, 2010, p. 38

3.7 Surplus Recycling Mechanism

Before the euro was established, Germany's persistent surplus in comparison with a country like Greece resulted in a gradual devaluation of the drachma relative to the Deutschmark. Thus balance was maintained, as the growing trade imbalances were cancelled out by differences in the exchange rates. However, once these very dissimilar nations (in economic terms) are unified under the same currency, something else is required to release the tension caused by unbalanced trade and capital flows. Varoufakis (2013) emphasizes the need for some mechanism for recycling surpluses from the surplus regions to the deficit regions, which is currently non-existent in the eurozone. Such recycling might come in the shape of transfers (e.g. paying unemployment benefits in one economic region through taxes raised in another) or in the form of productive and profitable investments in the deficit regions (e.g. building factories). In his own words:

> *In a sense, the reason why the dollar-zone (i.e. the United States) is a successful currency union whereas the eurozone is plagued with crises is that America features at least two surplus recycling mechanisms, whereas Europe boasts none. Indeed, without an effective surplus recycling mechanism in place, a currency union is bound to succumb to tectonic shifts, which eventually cause great cracks to form before finally the union shatters.*[11]

Since it is unlikely that such a recycling mechanism will ever materialize in Europe, we need to take a look at the real extent of this disparity (see the figure and table on the next page). While the current account balance of Germany has been constantly on the rise after the introduction of the euro, most other countries have not seen such consistent improvement. In fact, the situation became incredibly dire between 2007 and 2011 when the PIIGS and France experienced significant deficits in their current account balances, while Germany continued enjoying surpluses (see Table 4).

However, the positive thing to note here is that in the last few years, there has been an improving trend as many countries showed a positive balance in 2014. While the disparity remains high, it is certainly decreasing, so a recycling mechanism might not be so essential after all. For how long the situation keeps improving though, remains to be seen. In addition, one must

[11] See Varoufakis, 2013, p. 66

keep in mind that improving current account balances also gives out an indication of the undervaluation of the currency concerned. So, this may just as well act as another proof of the current soft currency status of the euro.

Figure 2 | Current Account Balance of Germany (as % of GDP from 1991 to 2013)

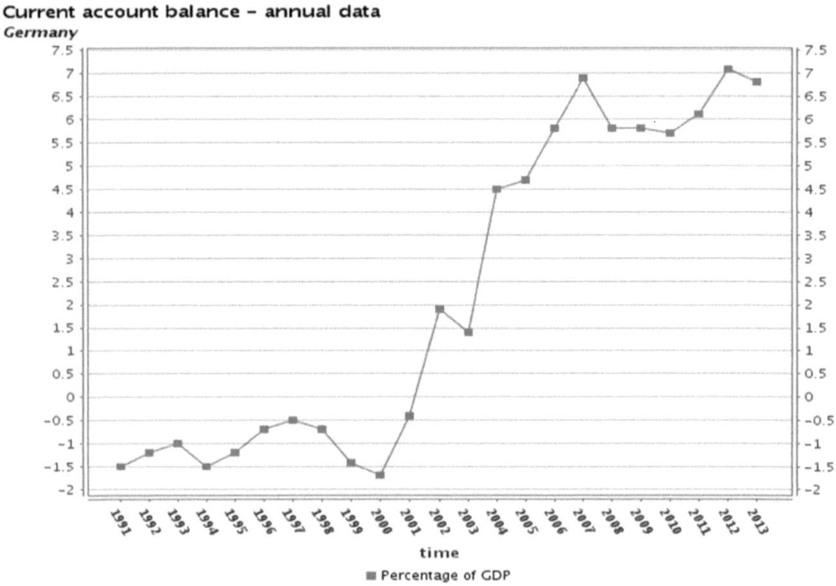

Source: Eurostat

Table 4 | Current Account Balances of Germany, France and PIIGS (percent of GDP)

Nation	1999	2007	2011	2014
Germany	-1.3	6.8	6.1	7.3
France	3.1	-0.3	-1.0	-0.9
Portugal	-8.1	-9.7	-6.0	0.1
Ireland	0.2	-6.1	-1.2	3.7
Italy	1.0	-1.5	-3.1	1.8
Greece	-5.1	-15.2	-9.9	-2.1
Spain	-2.9	-9.6	-3.2	1.0

Source: Deutsche Bank Research, Eurostat, Haver Analytics, World Bank

3.8 Sovereign Debt Crisis

When Greece entered the EMU, two main factors contributed to generating excessive deficits. First of all, Greece's drachma was a weaker currency when it switched to the euro, so it was admitted at a much higher exchange rate. Considering the prevailing wage rate at the time, many workers thus became uncompetitive compared to the more highly capitalized workers from northern countries. In order to counter this problem, the Greek government decided to increase spending and provided subsidies, for instance, in the form of early retirement schemes or unemployment benefits. Not only did such counter-measures have a negative impact on productivity, it also resulted in higher future deficits. Secondly, admission into the EMU meant that the ECB accepted Greek government bonds as collateral, and this backing from the ECB made Greece more complacent with regards to keeping the deficit in check.

The typical Keynesian policy of deficit spending implemented by the Greeks soon resulted in the market having doubts about Greece's ability to repay its debts. In January of 2009, the rating agency S&P cut Greece's rating to an A− and this exacerbated the uncertainty further. Due to a lack of investors in such uncertain economic environment, there was a very high possibility that the government would have to default on its obligations if the ECB stopped accepting Greek bonds as collateral for loans. Needless to say, the problems associated with this lack of confidence in sovereign bonds quickly began to spread, and so it came as no big surprise when in April 2009, the EU Commission started investigating excessive deficits in other countries like France, Ireland and Spain.

In October 2009, the newly elected government of Greece announced that the country's true deficit was in excess of 12% of national income, rather than the projected 6.5% (already more than double the Maastricht limit). As soon as the news came out, the interest rate the Greek state had to pay to borrow in order to refinance its EUR 300 billion debt increased rapidly (Varoufakis, 2013). By January 2010, it became evident that the Greek government was on the verge of defaulting, and before the end of the month, financial markets started selling Greek bonds at a faster pace after the Deutsche Bank warned that Greece's default would be more disastrous than the previous defaults of Argentina in 2001 or Russia in 1998 (Bagus, 2010). The

Deutsche Bank was concerned because it owned significant Greek government debt and there was the risk that a default could bring down the whole European banking system.

The EU started to discuss rescue packages, not only for Greece, but also for Portugal and Spain. A default of Portuguese and Spanish debtors would have negatively affected Germany, and especially French banks, due to their high levels of exposure in the crisis-inflicted countries. Due to its relatively higher exposure, the French government naturally had more interest in a bailout than the German government, as illustrated below:

Figure 3 | Bank Exposure (in billion $ at the end of March, 2011)

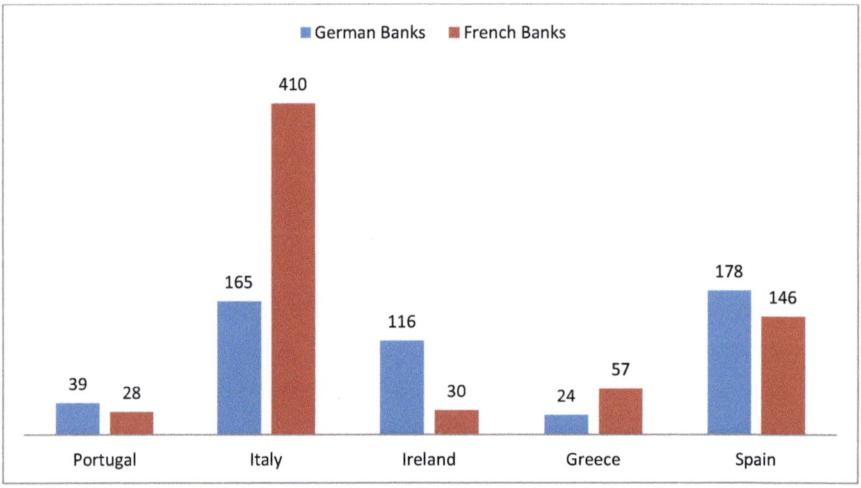

Source: BIS (2011)

On the other hand, the German government's main fear was a complaint of unconstitutionality. A bailout would violate article 125 of the Treaty on the functioning of the European Union, which states that member countries are not responsible for debts of other states. Most importantly, the German population voiced their opinion against a bailout.

In the mean time, problems of the banking system grew. The price of government bonds had been falling, and selling such bonds would reveal significant losses and further reduction of confidence in governments. The banking system and the government sector were more inter-connected than ever before, so the fear of systemic risk developed. It was feared that bankruptcy of any one of them could lead to the default of others. For example, a default of Portuguese banks or its government could, in turn, take down Spanish banks that held significant Portuguese debt. (BIS, 2010)

Since defaults of Greek and Spanish banks would have had adverse effects on German and French banks, it was only a matter of time before bailout packages were provided for troubled governments. Unable to roll over expiring debt and threatened by bankruptcy, the Greek government in April 2010 received a combined total of €110 billion in financial assistance with EMU member states providing €80 billion and the IMF covering the remaining €30 billion, under an adjustment programme, whereby the Greek government agreed to cut public wages, pensions and raise the sales tax. However, instead of bringing the situation under control, the emergency rescue package for Greece immediately led to fears of bankruptcy of a number of EMU states, and a subsequent collapse of the euro. Therefore, in May 2010, only shortly after the launch of the Greek programme, EMU member governments decided on the creation of a further €750 billion support fund for nations cut off from market funding. The EU commission provided €60 billion for the package, and it was agreed that once these funds were exhausted, countries could get loans guaranteed by the member states of up to €440 billion. Member states would guarantee loans based on their capital in the ECB. For instance, Germany would guarantee up to €123 billion. The remaining funds came from IMF, which would provide loans of up to €250 billion.

Meanwhile, as expected, most of the European economies suffered from recession. In 2008-09, Germany's GDP fell by 5%, while France experienced a decline of 2.6%. Similarly, among the PIIGS, Ireland's GDP declined by 7.1% and Spain's by 3.5%.[12]

As Bagus (2010) rightly points out, the overall ramification of this scenario was that the credibility of the ECB reduced substantially and confidence in the euro's capacity to serve as a store of value was also shaken. The primary goal of the ECB should have been to focus on maintaining a stable value of the euro, but instead it became susceptible to political interests.

[12] See Varoufakis, 2013, p. 175-176

During the course of the crisis, the ECB announced that it would start purchasing government bonds on the primary market, despite the fact that according to its statutes, the ECB must not buy government bonds directly from the issuer. This provision was meant to safeguard against central bank funding of government deficits. Such funding is frowned upon, particularly in Germany, ever since the German hyperinflation in the 1920s. So, there was a lot of opposition to the decision of buying government bonds, most notably from some former Bundesbankers.

Nevertheless, the ECB significantly stepped up its government bond purchases for the purpose of easing funding constraints faced by sovereign banks and borrowers. Apart from the change in the viewpoint of the ECB towards a more inflationary central bank, another factor adversely affected the quality of the euro, namely, qualitative easing (Bagus & Schiml, 2009). Qualitative easing is a shift in the composition of a central bank's assets towards less liquid and more risky assets, holding constant the size of the balance sheet. These assets can be sovereign instruments as well as private securities. So, in other words, it is a monetary policy used by central banks that leads to a reduction in the average quality of the assets backing the monetary base. By accepting problematic government bonds of troubled countries and private securities as collateral in repos and its marginal lending facility, the ECB had used qualitative easing to prop up the banking system, thereby diminishing the quality of euro (Buiter, 2008)

On the other hand, Quantitative Easing (QE) is an increase in the size of a central bank's balance sheet through a rise in its base money, holding constant the composition of its assets. The Federal Reserve's first quantitative easing program began in November 2008, and in simple terms, QE increases the money supply to inflate asset prices. Bastasin (2012) elaborates on how a central bank can maintain monetary stimulus through the process of QE by acquiring longer-term government securities, once the short-term rate of interest is very close to zero, and there is little room to push it further downwards. Theoretically, as soon as the economy recovers, the central bank should sell back the government securities and demonetize the public debt. However, it is reasonable to assume that markets would then demand higher interest rates to absorb a public debt that might have grown substantially during the recession. Under these circumstances, a government-controlled central bank would keep on buying treasury securities, thereby expanding the monetary base even further. Besides the risk of hyperinflation, this extreme form of monetary accommodation also creates an unstable scenario for long-term investments in industrial activities, and brings about a sense of uncertainty for households that rely on their savings.

In January 2015, the ECB announced that it will embark on a fully-fledged quantitative easing program from March 2015, whereby the bank will buy €1.14 trillion in government debt, which breaks down to a figure of €60 billion per month.[13] The decision to indulge in such a QE program means a further devaluation of the euro. QEs have been largely criticized for not delivering any real benefits to ordinary people, since the money flows into the bond market and does not add to the direct spending power of the general public.

Overall, QE is a massive central bank experiment, so we are in unchartered waters, as there is no precedent for it. QE has raised expectations among investors in the stock market and financial arena that the central banks would not let the markets go down. The general perception is that money will be pumped in and that will protect stocks from going down. This is a dangerous incentive to create as it causes the stocks to go shooting upwards. When a central bank eventually tries to unwind QE, it will be impossible to prevent the markets from overreacting. The removal of the stimulus will be a signal for the markets to go down. Low interest rates and QE has not created any real sustainable economic growth but the irony is that even though these policies have not worked, the central banks are still stubbornly sticking with them.

3.9 Summary

So, let us now recap the main points from this chapter:

- When governments wish to spend more than they receive in taxes, they issue bonds, and banks buy such bonds from the government because they know that they can be used as collateral. The ECB then accepts the bond (as collateral) in a reverse transaction, thereby lending money to the banks.

---

[13] See "ECB announces milestone €1.14 trn 'easy money program," Jan 22, 2015. Available at: https://www.rt.com/business/225111-ecb-announces-qe-draghi/

- The reputation of the Bundesbank and its sound money policies always got priority over political and other matters, before the ECB came into existence. France's desire to bring an end to the monetary dominance of the Bundesbank was the most important motive behind the campaign for EMU.
- As per the Maastricht Treaty, national central banks or the ECB were not allowed to directly finance government budget deficits of any kind, and the treaty also had a no bailout clause. However, both these stipulations were violated during the sovereign debt crisis. In fact, there were around seventy cases of violations of the 3 percent deficit threshold that could not possibly be justified by the economic downturn. Since the commencement of the crisis, none of the PIIGs along with Germany and France have managed to bring the government debt level down to anywhere near the 60% threshold.
- The major benefit of having a single currency is that exchange rate risks within the union are eliminated. A common currency can help to stimulate trade, enhance investment, and reduce uncertainty. The monetary union was also established to avoid a repetition of the devastating world wars. However, problems arise when it comes to quantifying the impact of these advantages. Lower transaction costs, greater price transparency, and stable exchange rates have little value without economic and financial stability.
- A big disadvantage of joining the monetary union is the loss of an independent monetary policy. The loss of the variable exchange rate as an economic policy tool is yet another drawback, as member countries of a currency union cannot use the option of devaluation to regain competitiveness.
- When Greece entered the EMU, two factors contributed to generating excessive deficits. First of all, Greece was admitted at a much higher exchange rate as the drachma was a weaker currency when it switched to the euro, resulting in loss of competitiveness. Secondly, admission into the EMU meant that the ECB accepted Greek government bonds as collateral, which made Greece even more complacent.
- Finally, the typical Keynesian policy of deficit spending implemented by the Greeks soon resulted in the market having doubts about Greece's ability to repay its debts. By January 2010, it became evident that the Greek government was on the verge of defaulting. The EU decided to provide stimulus packages, in the process violating article 125 of the Treaty, and intensifying the problem of moral hazard.

Chapter 4: Impending Demise of the Euro

Having discussed the sovereign debt crisis at length, it definitely raises some very important questions. Have we already reached the point of no return? Can the crisis-ridden financial system be brought under control? Is the demise of the euro just a matter of time? This section is dedicated to answering the aforementioned questions.

Just to recap, as Austrian business cycle theory explains, the credit expansion of the banking system caused an unsustainable boom. The theory goes that once the bubble bursts, the malinvestments must be liquidated. The liquidation is beneficial in the sense that it gets rid of inefficient projects and realigns the structure of production according to consumer preferences. Misused factors of production can then be transferred to more desirable projects.

In addition to the unsustainable credit-induced boom, the debt levels in society increased significantly. Credit expansion results in a debt level that would not be possible if money was backed by something like gold. Debts increase beyond the level justified because interest rates on the debts are low, thereby providing the incentive to borrow more than necessary. The fact that new debts may be created out of thin air to replace old ones exacerbates the problem. Overall, the current banking system enhances both private and government debts.

While the boom and over-indebtedness occurred on a worldwide scale, the European boom had certain characteristics of its own. Due to the introduction of the euro, interest rates fell in the high inflationary countries even though savings did not increase. The fixation of exchanges rates brought about by the euro also benefitted the traditionally high-inflation countries. These countries saw their debt burden reduced, which in turn encouraged more private and public consumption spending. Durable consumer goods such as houses were bought, leading to housing booms, the most notable of which occurred in Spain. Peripheral countries (PIIGs and other southern European countries) lost competitiveness as wage rates kept increasing. Overconsumption and the loss in competitiveness were sustained for a long period of time by means of enlarged private and public debts, and the inflow of new money created by the banking system.

The European boom affected countries in different ways. Malinvestments and over-consumption were higher in the high-inflation countries, but lower in countries like Germany, where savings rate had remained higher. In any case, everything soon fell apart when the boom came to its inevitable end. Declining house prices and bad loans caused severe problems in almost all the countries.

In Europe, the business model of maturity mismatching, whereby banks borrow short and lend long, proved to be a toxic combination when confidence eroded and short-term credit vanished. Bagus & Howden (2011) explains this model in the following way:

> *Normally, long-term interest rates are higher than the corresponding short-term rates. A bank that sells short-term rates (borrows money short-term), while buying long-term rates (investing money long-term) may profit from the difference (the "spread") between short-and long-term rates. Yet while maturity mismatching can turn out to be profitable, it is also very risky, because the short-term debts require continual reinvestment (that is there must be continual "rollover").*

When combined with credit expansion, maturity mismatching[14] can breed malinvestment. As credit expansion improves the likelihood that loans taken out at the present time can be easily renewed in the future, significant short-term borrowing will be undertaken to fund longer-term loans. Thus, it fosters an ever-riskier situation whereby illiquid long-term loans may make the banking system insolvent should an event arise where the short-term loans cannot be renewed, a situation that has been called "sudden stop syndrome" (Guillermo, 1998). When the perception of risk goes up, the likelihood that short-term loans will be discontinued also increases, creating an unsustainable situation for those banks that find themselves with a mismatched loan portfolio.

Now, let us consider the economic effects of maturity mismatching. The most obvious effect is that it can lead to instability in the banking system. Lenders do not want to renew short-term debt when liquidity declines too much, thereby making a maturity-mismatched bank illiquid. This problem can then spread rapidly to the whole financial system. Illiquid banks are forced to sell assets as a countermeasure to their funding shortfalls, which results in a decline of

[14] For a detailed examination of the economics of maturity mismatching see Philipp Bagus, "Austrian Business Cycle Theory: Are 100 Percent Reserves Sufficient to Prevent a Business Cycle?" Libertarian Papers 2, No. 2 (2010). See Bagus and Howden, "The Legitimacy of Loan Maturity Mismatching," for the ethical aspects of this practice.

asset prices. When such a situation arises, banks face insolvency, as they have to write down capital. This in turn, may tempt other market participants to stop rolling over loans to banks, leading to a panic. Bagus & Howden (2011) notes that during a panic, the long-term assets can only be sold at a considerably lower price and so bank losses grow. Liquidity problems spread like wildfire and banks liquidate further assets to cover significant losses. A cycle develops, leading to further liquidations and price declines. In this way, trust in the banking system evaporates and it may eventually collapse.

When these maturity-mismatched banks triggered a crisis in Europe, the unsound financial institutions should have been liquidated. However, the available free-market solutions to the banks' solvency problems were not implemented, and instead governments decided to inject capital into banks. Since raising taxes is not a popular option among politicians, these government injections were financed by increasing public debt. Not only did such government interventions delay the recovery, but the enlargement of public debts also places a huge burden on the European welfare states. Unsustainable government debts can lead to the collapse of smaller welfare states, in the not-too-distant future.

As we have already discussed, when the euro was brought into existence, it was implicitly assumed among member nations that no nation would leave the single currency after joining it. If things went downhill, a nation could be rescued by the rest of the EMU. Access to cheap credit allowed countries like Greece to ignore structural problems and maintain a gigantic public sector, as they held on to the belief that any deficits could be financed by money creation on the part of the ECB, externalizing the costs to fellow EMU members.

Moreover, when the crisis erupted, there was always the risk that contagions from Greece could threaten other countries that have extremely high debts or deficits, such as Portugal, Italy, and Spain. This risk still persists today. In addition, some of these countries suffer from inflexible labor markets and high unemployment. If these countries get infected, it could lead to their insolvency, and the breakdown of the euro.

According to Varoufakis (2013), the crisis in Europe has set in motion certain forces that are tearing the eurozone apart, setting the surplus economies, with Germany at the helm, against the peripheral countries, whose structural deficits cannot be cured easily, regardless of the austerity measures being put in place. The European economies are stagnating, mainly due to the inability to coordinate policy at some central level, consequently shattering the dream of a political union.

Many people wonder how it is possible that despite the central banks increasing base money to extraordinary levels, we have had so little inflation (based on official figures), in the past few years. The main reason behind this is that most of the European economies are structurally damaged, so the additional money in circulation cannot be put to effective use. Most European companies are not short of finance, so there is no financial constraint. Lowering the cost of finance is not making them invest any more in productive projects; rather it is pushing them into speculative assets that will have problems later on. Money has only gone to the stock market and not into the economic system as a whole, so we have not seen prices rising in a broad way.

In relation to financial crisis and depression, Charles Kindleberger identified the theory of *regime uncertainty* which holds that even when interest rates have declined sufficiently to attract investors back into the economy, investors may still refrain from doing so, because indecisive public policy makes it impossible to calculate returns with any degree of accuracy. Regime uncertainty refers to the added uncertainty caused by government policies seemingly designed to improve conditions that typically ends up making things worse (Rickards, 2014). The easy money policy pioneered by the Fed and ECB has clearly provided us with such a scenario.

Thomas Palley, prominent economist and author, explained precisely how Financialization is wrecking havoc in the European economies. Financialization is a situation in which the financial sector increasingly starts to dominate the economy. More and more of the profit share, instead of going to industries and production of goods and services gets redirected by means of the financial sector. Instead of profits, things get converted into debt and more of the payments to capital get paid back in the form of interest. So, rather than being long term players, manufacturing products and building huge industries with one eye on the future, short term profits gets the priority. For instance, we see that in terms of how CEOs are compensated with stock options. The only thing they are interested in is pumping up the share prices, rather than growing a company that is going to produce income and jobs, long into the future. Financialization of the economy is really an asset based economy dependent on bubbles to fuel growth. Moreover, Financialization captures all the three dimensions of ideas, politics and the economy on behalf of the affluent people. This is how Financialization distorts economies all over the world. One must also keep in mind that a single crash does not immediately lead to another; there is a period of stagnation in between. This is the phase we are currently going through. To counter stagnation, issues like income and wealth distribution, demographics, and slowdown in technological advancement has to be addressed.

Coming back to the ECB, it introduced negative interest rates and cheap long-term loans in June, 2014. The ECB cut its deposit rates from zero to negative 0.1% all in an effort to encourage banks to lend more to households and businesses. This made it the first central bank to use a negative rate. Banks sitting on a lot of excess reserves were depositing them with the ECB at 0%. Once negative interest rates were introduced, they started paying a marginal penalty of a one-tenth of a point. There are some potential downsides to this that have not been addressed enough. One thing is that costs are being thrown back at the banking system. At 0% there was nothing either way, but now that there is what can be considered as a tax, presumably banks are going to pass that back on to depositors, or conceivably it could be passed on to lenders. So, this gives rise to a paradoxical situation. Low investment in Europe is the result of regulations and political uncertainties, so negative interest rates would do nothing to improve the situation. All it does is add to the financial fragility in the system. In such a case, sensing the impending collapse of the currency, expecting people to move away from fiat money to commodities like gold and silver cannot be thought of as an absurd proposition any longer.

The charts on the next couple of pages illustrate the low levels of interest rates persisting worldwide. Figure 4 depicts the downhill trend in the EONIA index (EONIA stands for Euro Overnight Index Average). Figure 5 shows that the Federal Reserve lowered its borrowing rate an incredible 5.5 percent during the boom, while the ECB also lowered its rate by 2.75 percent, giving rise to the adverse effects we are witnessing today. Figure 6 portrays the fact that the interest rate has already gone into negative territory in the eurozone and Japan, while the rates in the U.S.A. and U.K. are hovering dangerously close to the same region.

Figure 4 | EONIA (Jan 2012 – Jan 2016)

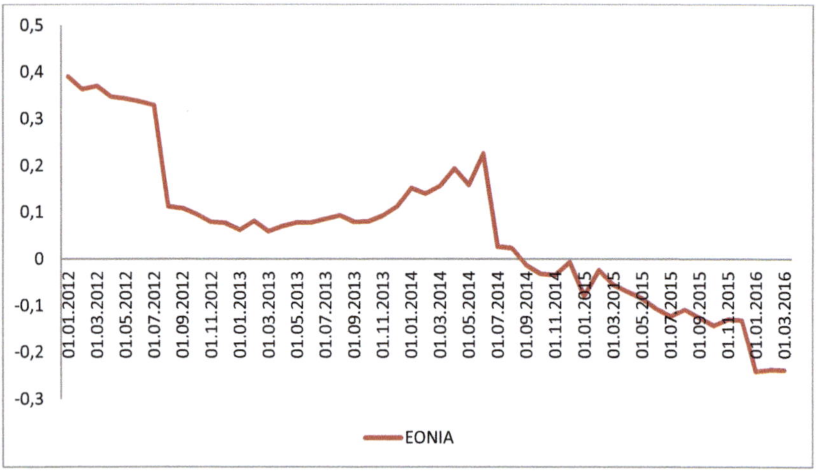

Source: Bloomberg

Figure 5 | Interest Rate Comparison between Euro Area and USA (2000 -2015)

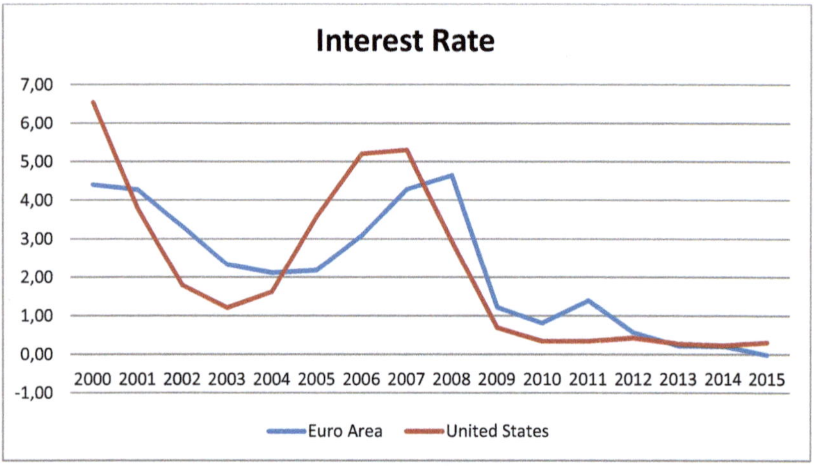

Source: Eurostat

Figure 6 | Key Target Central Bank Interest Rates (Jan 2009 – Apr 2016)

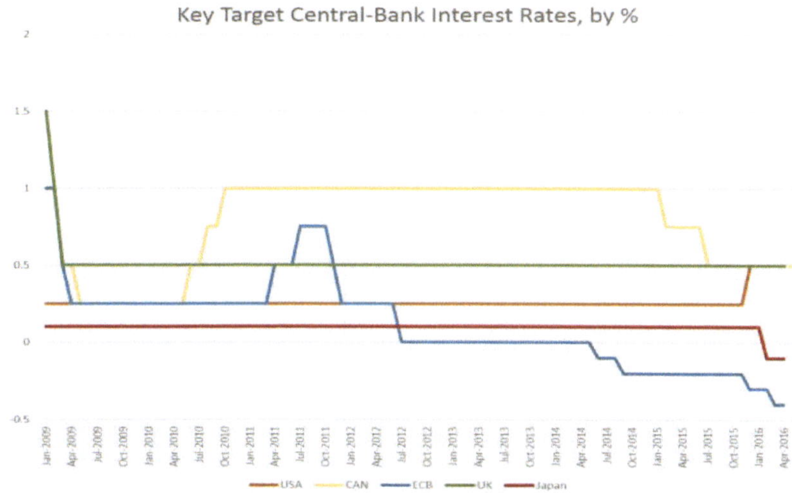

Source: Mises Institute

Now, let us move on from low interest rates to what happens when a currency loses its purchasing power. Collapse of money occurs due to a loss of confidence in the future purchasing power of the currency. It leads to the holders dumping the currency, either by means of spending faster or through the acquisition of hard assets. This drastic behavioral change results in higher interest rates and inflation. Rickards (2014) mentioned that the international monetary system has already collapsed three times in the last century – in 1914, 1939 and 1971; so this is not something new and another episode is certainly possible. Each collapse was followed by a turbulent period. The First and Second World Wars contributed to the earlier collapses, while U.S. president Nixon's decision to abandon gold convertibility, led to the collapse of 1971, which was followed by widespread confusion, culminating in the near collapse of the dollar in 1978.

The problem with policymakers is that they use some equilibrium models and think that if inflation is not high enough, nominal GDP is not sufficient. By relying on such equilibrium models, they believe that they can print money, create some inflation, get nominal GDP on a sustainable path, then withdraw policy and replace nominal with real GDP. In fact, the world we live in today is a complex system and such a system is characterized by sudden, sharp changes that mathematical models does not take into consideration. So, it is possible to continue printing money without restraints, but then suddenly confidence may disappear. When confidence in a currency is weakened due to central bank policy or other issues, people will look for other safe havens. Paul Volcker, Chairman of the Federal Reserve from 1979 to 1987, who is widely credited with adopting strict inflation-averse policies (the only Fed Chairman to do so in recent times) that brought inflation under control in the U.S.A., was right in his assertion that confidence is indispensible to the stability of a currency. Unfortunately, nowadays the policymakers take confidence for granted and this complacency runs the risk of slowly but surely destroying national economies in the future.

Inflation is the stealth destroyer of savings, capital, and economic growth. Inflation often begins indiscernibly and gains substantial momentum before the general public finally starts to experience its ill-effects. Rickards (2014) notes that this lag in comprehension is the essence of what is called money illusion, a phrase that refers to a perception that real wealth is being created. Only later is it discovered that bankers and shrewd investors captured the wealth, while the general population is left with devalued savings and pensions. Inflation also results in the rise of nominal prices of stocks and real estate, instilling in the minds of people an illusion of wealth creation, thereby covering up the fact that the real purchasing power of their assets is actually declining. The fact that prices rise in various stages is the reason behind inflation initially remaining invisible, despite large bouts of credit creation. A lot hinges on how the newly created money actually enters the system and where it is spent first. Generally, inflation can be more noticeable in financial assets than in consumer prices, as was the case during the stock market bubble in the 1990s or the more recent real estate boom. Some of the newly printed money also goes overseas, courtesy of international trade, which is then converted to local currencies. However, most of this money remains on deposit in central banks, thus deferring the impact on domestic prices (Schiff & Downes, 2009). The following table depicts the scenario explained above:

Figure 7 | Average Price Inflation in Germany and PIIGS

	Germany	Portugal	Ireland	Italy	Greece	Spain
1994-1998	1,1	3,2	1,8	3,5	5,9	3,3
1999-2007	1,6	3,1	3,4	2,3	3,2	3,1
2007-2011	1,8	2,4	0,8	2,2	3,3	2,4
2012-2014	1,5	1	0,9	1,6	-0,4	1,2

Source: Deutsche Bank Research, ECB, Eurostat, Haver Analytics

As we can see, there has been a general declining trend in inflation rates (except in the case of Germany where inflation stayed relatively constant) over the years. This gives us a good indication that asset inflation has been greater than price inflation in recent years. So, focusing only on trying to keep price inflation rates low by way of inflation targeting while ignoring the dangers of asset inflation, adds up to a doomed policy measure. Simply worrying about deflation and neglecting asset inflation can lead to disastrous consequences, which we will discuss in the forthcoming chapters.

Moreover, behavioral psychology provides us with a reason to believe that inflation targeting is not beneficial. It is worth noting that if the monetary central planners were to succeed with their goal and maintain two percent average annual price inflation in the eurozone, this would mean that over a twenty-year period the purchasing power of euro would decline by around 50 percent (Ebeling, 2015) According to Rickards (2014), human nature dictates that once the inflation target is achieved and expectations are altered, a feedback loop will emerge where inflation expectations will keep on getting higher. It would not be possible for central banks to contain this feedback loop because its dynamic is a function of human nature, and not of monetary policy.

In international trade, strong (hard) and weak (soft) currencies can be both good as well as bad, depending on the scenario. For instance, a weak currency is bad for consumers in the home country because it makes the purchase of imported goods costlier and traveling abroad more expensive. A devalued currency means that the currency can be used to exchange fewer units of another country's currency. On the other hand, a soft currency is good news for export-oriented industries, because it makes their products cheaper to foreigners and hence much easier to sell. Naturally, the opposite is true for a strong currency. One thing that policymakers do not seem adept to grasp properly is that currency devaluation as a path to increased exports is not as simplistic as it is made out to be. Rickards (2011) points out that such depreciation may lead to higher input costs, tariffs, embargoes and a global recession sooner rather than later. Currency devaluation actually hinders proper recovery. A strong, stable currency is a catalyst for expanding trade and acts as a magnet for investment. Inflation and currency devaluation is to a large extent the same thing in terms of the effects they have on an economy. While the beneficial side of enhanced exports is always highlighted, the fact that it also makes imports of raw materials and other inputs more costly is largely ignored.

The Federal Reserve of the United States was established it 1913 with the most important mandate being to maintain the purchasing power of the dollar. However, since 1913, the dollar has lost over 95 percent of its value.[15] Taking into consideration only the past 20 years as the relevant timeframe, America is already witnessing its third stock bubble, and its second housing bubble. When these bubbles burst, the world economy will be confronted with a worse panic than what occurred in 2008, and the pleas for a further round of bailouts would not be lagging far behind.

Inflation is also getting a bit of traction lately in the USA and that is a reason why the Federal Reserve is talking about tightening monetary policy by cutting down on QE, and hoping to eventually return to more normal rates. However, since the Fed has waited too long to increase rates, now we have reached a point where the financial system is completely reliant on constant

[15] See Rickards, 2011, p. 183

government intervention (applicable worldwide). Massive budget deficits and spending can only run on low interest rates. So, we should get ready for the next recession to hit, and hopefully with the right policies, things will get back to normal again, at least in terms of interest rates. Rickards (2011) also correctly suggests that the value of a nation's currency is its Achilles' heel. Bonds, stocks, and other investments are all priced in a nation's currency. The bottom line is that if the central bank carries on this charade of money printing, the ultimate result may turn out to be the destruction of the currency. If the currency is destroyed, all markets will go down with it, ultimately leading to the demise of the nation.

According to Eichengreen (2011), a currency's stability is the first thing that exporters and importers, as well as investors take a look at, before determining a future course of action. Due to the fact that the US dollar is the world's reserve currency, only extreme financial mismanagement by the United States could precipitate a flight from the dollar. However, the recent financial crisis gives us a warning that such serious mismanagement is something that cannot be ruled out.

So, an impending collapse of the dollar is certainly a possibility, in the medium to long term. Trapped between a choice of higher interest rates that would undoubtedly bring about a recession and lower rates that could result in the level of inflation going out of control, the government has opted to present a facade of well-being that is ultimately unsustainable. It has only allowed fundamental weaknesses to worsen. The Fed is now caught in no man's land with inflation on one side and recession on the other side, and sadly it is too late to prevent the dire consequences of either (Schiff & Downes, 2009).

What is applicable in the case of the dollar may prove to be even more applicable for the euro. James Rickards, prominent American lawyer, explains the relationship between the euro and dollar using an appropriate analogy:

> *The euro and dollar are best understood as two passengers on the same ship. At any given time, one passenger may be on a higher deck and the other on a lower one. They can change places at will and move higher or lower relative to each other, but at the end of the day they are on the same vessel moving at the same speed heading for the same destination. The day-to-day fluctuations reflect technical factors, short-term supply and demand requirements, fears of*

default or disintegration of the euro followed quickly by relief at the latest rescue or bailout package. Through it all, the euro-dollar pair travel on, never separated by more than the dimensions of the vessel on which they both sail.[16]

So, now coming back to the discussion regarding Europe again, experts had previously warned that a common currency backed by a single central bank would be incompatible with the diverse fiscal policies of the member countries adopting the euro. Countries that had been reckless in terms of spending, or historically devalued their currencies, such as Greece, would be awkward partners in a union that included fiscally prudent nations like Germany. These flaws were there from the beginning, but unfortunately it took ten long years for them to be fully revealed.

Rickards (2011) argues further that the bureaucrats in Brussels have built a win-win situation for themselves by turning a blind eye to the recklessness. They know that the success of the euro project would be hailed, if the sovereign debt crisis somehow resolved itself. In the case of the more likely scenario of a failure, the policymakers' solution would be more, rather than less supervision from Brussels. So, in short, if the euro succeeded they won praise and if the euro came under stress they won power.

The calamitous situation we currently find ourselves in was launched by the erroneous decisions of the political class. Financial markets and credit rating agencies have assisted in accelerating the development further. The measures undertaken to prevent the demise of the euro are pointless and will eventually prove to be an unaffordable battle against the markets that cannot be won. Countries within the monetary union having a solid economic footing, especially Germany, are now caught in the euro trap. Under the political scenario prevailing nowadays, these countries have no choice but to put up with new rescue packages for crisis-ridden countries and to tolerate the purchase of bonds by the ECB, despite knowing well enough that such means of financing member states is not compatible with the European Treaties. Moreover, strict austerity measures that are imposed on the recipient countries in exchange for loans and guarantees are not entirely effective because the countries participating in the monetary union are sovereign nations. Therefore, it is extremely difficult to control their budgetary and financial issues solely by means of outside pressure. Imposing sanctions would also be counter-productive

[16] See Rickards, 2011, p. 124-125

as an option to bring the situation under control as it will only ensure increased hardship on the already troubled economies.

Brown (2012) points out that if German or French citizens had been told back in the early 1990s that the formation of EMU could make them responsible for financing rescue packages to aid weaker members, the whole project would probably have been rejected outright. Truth be told, German citizens were never given an opportunity to vote in a referendum, and in France the referendum held in 1992 only came down in favor of EMU by a small margin.

In any case, the attempt to manipulate the market through interventions such as the purchase of government bonds by the ECB is ultimately doomed to failure. A country must pursue a stability oriented policy to enhance its creditworthiness in capital markets and lower its refinancing cost. Only by adopting such a policy can a country regain confidence of potential investors and convince them of its long-term solvency.

So overall, it can be said that the euro triggered the crisis in Europe. The single currency has not only allowed the peripheral countries of the euro area to live beyond their means, but has also shattered their international competitiveness. The outcome was a massive increase in debt of the countries concerned. As these members of the EMU faced the threat of bankruptcy and were no longer able to refinance on favorable terms in the capital markets, the ECB along with the international community stepped in with rescue packages, which not only violated the terms of the European treaties, but also exacerbated the problems. Ultimately, due to the inherent fundamental flaws in the euro, it would be hard to prevent the EMU from disintegrating. A breakup of the monetary union is definitely a plausible scenario in the medium term. Needless to say, it would bring with it a lot of negative economic and social consequences in Europe, and far beyond its borders. What we are experiencing now is simply the calm before the storm. Therefore, the concerned countries would be well-advised to heed the warning and be prepared, when the storm finally hits.

Chapter 5: The Deutschmark

Before the introduction of the euro, the Bundesbank set a high standard in terms of a hard currency. It is true that the Bundesbank did inflate the money supply, but it printed new money at a far slower rate compared to the high inflationary policies of southern European countries, which used their central banks to finance deficits in an unrestrictive manner. According to Bagus (2010), comparisons with the Bundesbank clearly exposed the shortcomings of the governments of high-inflation countries. Introducing the euro helped to put to bed these embarrassing comparisons and devaluations, as will be discussed shortly.

In reality, a majority of the German population wanted to keep the Deutschmark (DM). However, in order to convince the skeptical general public, German politicians used the argument that the single currency was necessary for maintaining peace in Europe. They did not have it all their way though because some German academics countered by pointing out the long-term dangers that the euro poses for Germany, and urged the government not to sign the Maastricht Treaty. Also, many legal experts raised constitutional concerns about the Maastricht Treaty. However, later on the German constitutional court gave its verdict that the Maastricht Treaty was constitutional. Most importantly though, the court noted that Germany could only participate provided there is a stable currency, and would have to leave the monetary union if it turned out to be unstable. So, this gives Germany the right to leave the single currency in the future, if it proves to be unsustainable. Last but not least, many Bundesbankers were against the euro from the beginning and argued vehemently that a political union should be achieved first, before a common currency is adopted.

Now, after joining the monetary union, Germany finds itself in a disadvantageous position because the thing which works in favor of the not-so-prudent countries is that southern Europe has more control over the ECB. The council of the ECB comprises of the presidents of the respective national central banks, and the directors of the ECB. They all have the same vote. This means that Germany and other hard currency countries such as the Netherlands and Austria hold the minority of votes against countries like France, Greece, Italy, Portugal, and Spain, whose governments are less averse to deficits (Bagus, 2010).

So, a question may arise as to why Germany gave up the Deutschmark in the first place. To answer this, first and foremost, one has to take into account the fact that the Bundesbank frequently created pressure on other nations to curtail their printing presses or to realign their foreign exchange rates. In contrast, France's own central bank was under the direct control of its government and was used as an instrument to pay for government expenditures. The Bank of France wanted to enhance growth by means of credit expansion. The Bundesbank acted as a hindrance to these endeavors, and since the more independent Bundesbank did not inflate to the same extent, France had to devalue several times. The DM set a high standard as a stable currency, mainly thanks to the resistance of the German public towards inflation and its independence from government monetary interferences. When the Bundesbank raised interest rates, the Bank of France had to follow suit if it did not want the Franc to depreciate, and hence had to realign. France knew that in a common central bank, Germany would be in the minority, which could open up the possibility for French politicians to determine its course. So, Löffler (2010) argues that Germany ultimately had to give up the Deutschmark and monetary sovereignty in exchange for unification. France's political elite wanted to establish a single currency mainly to ensure that the DM does not become too powerful, and also to shore up its already important banking sector, both of which they eventually managed to accomplish.

5.1 Agenda 2010

Unlike most other eurozone members, Germany did pursue structural changes to its economy soon after the turn of the century, focusing specially on its labor markets. Following reunification, Germany's economic performance was gloomy. According to Overtveldt (2011), the country's growth lagged behind that of most other EMU members. Unemployment shot up from 7.5 percent in 1992 to 11.5 percent in 1997 and increased to nearly 12 percent by 2005. Germany's problems at the beginning of the twenty-first century were to a considerable extent the result of entering the monetary union with an exchange rate that was too high.

By 2003, Chancellor Schroeder became convinced that comprehensive economic reform was needed if Germany wanted to hold a prestigious position among the most advanced industrial countries. Consequently, he launched an economic reform program dubbed 'Agenda 2010'. The goal was to improve the country's medium-term growth prospects and restore

Germany's international competitiveness. Mayer (2012) notes that this agenda was Germany's most comprehensive economic reform and restructuring program since the introduction of the 'Social Market Economy' by Germany's minister of economics, Ludwig Erhard, in the 1950s.

Schroeder's agenda included an overhaul of the social security system, ranging from the welfare to the pension system and a reform of labour market regulations. In addition, changes were made in the tax system by means of a reduction in business and income taxes, and the service sector was deregulated. Moreover, a reduction in welfare and unemployment benefits raised incentives to work. Overall, labour market reforms seemed to have played the biggest role in the restoration of the German economy's international competitiveness.

While these economic reforms were essential for the subsequent strong economic performance of the economy, they initially kept unemployment high, depressed real disposable income growth, and thus dampened domestic demand growth. In fact, the paltry growth that was attained during these years was mainly based on the strength of German exports, leading to a surge in Germany's current account surplus.

However, by 2006, Germany's economic growth turned out to be higher than the eurozone average. Its unemployment rate had declined to 7.2 percent by 2008, while the employment rate, or the percentage of the working-age population effectively employed, had risen from 69 percent in 2000 to 74 percent in 2008 (Overtveldt, 2011). Drastic and often painful structural adjustments were required for Germany's revival, which eventually made the nation the strongest economy in the eurozone.

5.2 German Stability Culture and Possible Exit from EMU

To most Germans, an economically stable environment means low inflation and financial stability. This view culminates directly from the bad memories of the economic, social, and political catastrophes that resulted from the 1920s hyperinflation in Germany. Former Chancellor Gerhard Schroeder made this abundantly clear when he claimed that "if you try to fight German stability culture, you are bound to lose. It's better not to start that game."[17] In fact, this culture of

[17] Schroeder as quoted in Marsh, 2009, p. 221

stability has found its way into Germany's constitution. The constitutional court in Karlsruhe, in its 1993 ruling on the Maastricht Treaty, defined "the aim of stability as the benchmark of the monetary union" and further, that "in the case the stability of the community fails, a dissociation (of Germany) from that community is warranted.[18] This ruling makes it crystal clear that leaving a destabilized European monetary union would present no legal problems for Germany.

The stability of the EMU's economic and financial environment will inevitably be undermined whenever member countries face financial instabilities. Needless to say, providing the necessary funding to assist these countries would weigh heavily on Germany's public finances, as well as its credit rating. So, it comes as no surprise that people have tried to address the situation, in recent years. Hans-Olaf Henkel, the former head of the Federation of German Industries, even argued that the present eurozone should be split up into a German-led hard-currency union and a southern group led by France that could devalue its currency to regain competitiveness (Henkel, 2010). Another proposal was put forward by Dieter Spethmann, former chairman of the steel conglomerate Thyssen, asking for an end of the euro in its present form and creating a northern euro.[19]

It is safe to say that concern for financial and monetary stability ranks high on the list of priorities for corporate Germany. Overtveldt (2011) suggests that adherence to this stability culture may end up dominating the concerns about corporate sales and competitiveness. In 2010, Thomas de Maziere, one of Germany's top politicians argued:

> *After 1990, Germany underwent a fundamental change. Until 1990, Germany was a divided country. It was economically strong but politically weak, and not really a fully sovereign state.... After 1990, not only the map of Germany but the map of Europe changed dramatically.... It may be new for Europe that Germany is representing its interests with new vigour.... The biggest net payer into the EU budget has to defend its interests.*[20]

Similarly, Katinka Barysch, director of Political Relations at Allianz, remarked:

[18] Ruling of the Constitutional Court as reprinted in Proissl, 2010, p. 15

[19] See interview with Spethmann in FAZ.NET, February 7, 2011

[20] De Maziere as quoted in *The Economist*, Charlemagne's Notebook, May 20, 2010.

"...perhaps for the first time since the second World War, [the Germans] are allowing themselves to be defiant and proud. Their export-oriented, stability-obsessed economic model is not up for discussion. Their participation in the Eurozone is becoming more conditional. Even the wisdom of the whole EU project is now sometimes questioned.... For the generation of Helmut Kohl, Europe was a matter of war and peace. For Merkel and most of her contemporaries, it is a question of costs and benefits." [21]

In addition, *The Economist* noted in 2010 that, "Germany has changed. The days of France having all the ideas and Germany paying all the bills are over."[22]

From a political standpoint, it is not a good omen that the general public has been so outraged by the policymakers' decision to use taxpayers' hard-earned money for the purpose of rescuing countries that lived beyond their means. So, this makes it highly unlikely that the funding will continue in the long run. Going down the path of continuously financing these troubled countries may at some point instigate a German exit from the monetary union.

5.3 Reverting to the Deutschmark

Let us now try to refute the claims made my critics against a move away from the euro towards the Deutschmark (DM).

5.3.1 Claim: Euro is stronger than the Deutschmark

The first thing to take into consideration when comparing the euro with the DM is that wage growth and interest rates during DM times were always above the rate of inflation in Germany. So people enjoyed welfare gains in the form of real income growth. In contrast, since the introduction of the euro, wages in Germany have fallen in real terms, at around 0.8 percent (between 2000 and 2011). In the lower income groups, a decrease of nearly 20 percent was recorded. Therefore, German consumers today have less income at their disposal, despite lower nominal inflation rates. In addition, the euro has had an adverse effect on savers due to the low interest rates brought about by the expansionary monetary policy of the ECB.

---

[21] See Barysch, 2010, p. 2, 3.

[22] See *The Economist*, Charlemagne's Notebook, May 20, 2010.

Money supply in the monetary union has increased by around 50% between 2000 and 2012, but the production potential has increased by only about 20 percent. The fact that this easy money policy pursued by the ECB has not yet found a significant increase in the cost of living is largely thanks to the pressure of international competition and the imports of cheap mass consumer goods from low-wage countries. However, this has certainly limited the scope for wage increases. The rise in money supply which has accelerated with the onset of the euro rescue packages in 2010 has had its consequences. The effect is visible on the financial markets, as in recent years there has been a significant increase in the prices of commodities, securities, and real estate. Such asset-inflation caused by the loose monetary policy of the ECB combined with the lack of real wage growth, is the main reason behind the gap between rich and poor in Germany growing wider, since 2000.[23]

5.3.2 Claim: Germany's export industry will collapse with DM

Few would argue against the fact that a new German Mark would appreciate against other currencies. Estimates range from 30 percent to 50 percent appreciation of the new currency. This may have an adverse impact on exports, as German goods and services would become more expensive abroad. Moreover, it is also argued that in the case of dissolution of the monetary union, German trade would decline with other countries of the eurozone.

Critics point out that for the above reasons, a return to DM would be economically devastating and many jobs in the domestic industry might be under threat. However, no one can reliably predict how much a new German Mark would actually appreciate after reintroduction. Nor is it clear whether the increase in value would be a long-lasting one or just a short-term thing. Some historical facts of the DM era can be used to counter the pessimism of the euro sympathizers. Between 1953 and 1999, the Federal Republic of Germany was consistently among the three leading exporting nations in the world, despite the fact that the DM was considered to be a high-value, hard currency throughout that period. Before each round of revaluation announced by the Bundesbank, politicians and economists alike, predicted significant

[23] See *Back to Deutschmark?*, European Alliance for Freedom, p. 4

declines in German exports, growth losses and high unemployment, but none of these things actually materialized.

On the contrary, Germany's exports improved after each appreciation of DM. At first glance this may come as a surprise to many, but studies have shown that the success of German products on the international markets is primarily owed to comparatively higher quality, goodwill, brand loyalty, as well as the innovative power and flexibility of German enterprises. Innovation and technology are the key elements associated with a robust export sector, and German companies such as SAP, Daimler and many others epitomize this. Furthermore, German companies often operate as world leading suppliers in niche markets. They manufacture products that other companies are not able to offer. So, the price for buyers only plays a secondary role, and thus exchange rate adjustments have little impact on export volumes. In fact, in some countries, people feel that the higher the price of the car, the more prestige is associated with it. For example, in a country like Bangladesh, owning a Mercedes or BMW is considered as a status symbol. So, people are prepared to pay huge amounts of money to own a German-made car.

Having said that, naturally as an export powerhouse, it comes with the territory that Germany would favor a weak euro to gain an edge in the currency wars. It is important to bear in mind that Germany is not only an external exporter, but also an internal exporter within the European Union. For these eurozone exports, there are no currency considerations since both the exporter and the importer use the same currency (Rickards, 2011). There is no denying the fact that the eurozone countries are still extremely important for German exports, but the importance of markets like China, India, and Russia has enlarged significantly in recent years. Needless to say, the more important these non-euro areas become for German exports, the less the export-oriented industries (along with their trade unions) will resist an exit from the monetary union. As German economist Jens Bastian commented: "In the corporate sector, shifting trade patterns may signal that Europe does not necessarily come first anymore for German businesses."[24]

Coming back to the historical aspect, as it turned out, a strong DM was quite beneficial for Germany's economy. Export-oriented companies were forced to constantly increase their productivity to stay competitive and optimize their product range. The strong DM thus managed

[24] Bastian in the *Financial Times*, January 17, 2011.

to bring about enhanced innovation and this had a positive long-lasting impact on profits, and created the necessary scope for increased productivity of the employees. After the collapse of the monetary system of Bretton Woods with its fixed exchange rates, the DM appreciated against the French franc by 30 percent, against the U.S. dollar by 40 percent and against the British pound as much as 50 percent, from 1969 to 1973. Despite that, German exports kept on growing stronger during this time period.[25]

Undeniably, a new, strong D-mark will make exports more expensive, but one must always keep in mind that it would also reduce the cost of imports coming into Germany. Therefore, an appreciation of the currency would have less of an impact on the profits of exporters, as it not only reduces an exporter's revenues but also lowers the cost of the exporter's imported inputs. Since a significant portion of German exported goods rely on raw materials imported from abroad, there would be a price dampening effect, which the companies could pass on to their foreign customers to offset currency-related cost increases. The main beneficiaries of a return to the DM would be the consumers in Germany. They would pay considerably less money for imported products because of the strong external value of the new currency. That would increase the purchasing power of consumers and stimulate domestic demand, thus opening up the scope for wage increases.

The expected increase in domestic demand after a return to the DM would also give Germany's trading partners the chance to sell more goods on the German market. This could enable them to reduce their large current account deficits with Germany. Of course, this can only happen if the euro is abolished and the national currencies are reintroduced in Europe. If such a scenario does come into existence, not only will the purchasing power of German consumers increase, but the price competitiveness of crisis-inflicted countries will also rise, since they will have the possibility to devalue their currencies again. These countries would then be in a position to export more goods, which in turn would also improve the sales opportunities for German companies in these foreign markets. Scientific studies show that if the gross domestic product of Germany's major trading partners' increase by one percent then German exports can increase by more than two percent. This effect would help to compensate for the export shock that the German economy might suffer from reintroducing a stronger DM.

[25] See *Back to Deutschmark?*, European Alliance for Freedom, p. 18

5.3.3 Claim: Europe will collapse if euro fails

From its inception the euro has been a political project, rather than an economic one. A common currency does not work without a strong political union and proper economic integration of the participating countries. The European political elites were aware of this issue from the beginning. However, the reluctance of states towards giving up their sovereignty in favor of a European political union has proven to be too strong.

The idea that the end of the euro would have disastrous consequences for the European project also does not hold much substance, from a historical perspective. The European cooperation took place for more than 40 years without a common currency. This cooperation would continue even if the euro is abolished. Moreover, cooperation with other European countries that do not belong to the monetary union is going on without difficulties for a long time. It is actually the single currency (and its shortcomings), which has revived the resentments among the various nations of the monetary union.

5.3.4 Claim: Reverting to DM could be costly

According to the figures published by the Munich Ifo Institute, the liability risk of Germany from the euro rescue amounts to 553 billion euro (as of 08/05/2015).[26] This is the sum German taxpayers would lose if the crisis-ridden countries of European periphery fail to pay back their debts to Germany. Thus, proponents of the euro argue that Germany must remain in the EMU because a withdrawal would probably prove to be more expensive. However, this argument is based on the assumption that the crisis-inflicted countries would eventually repay the debts owed. As we all know, this is easier said than done. Since peripheral countries cannot compensate their competitive disadvantages by unilateral currency adjustments, it would be extremely difficult for them to regain the level of competitiveness required to repay all the debts. The only alternative to counter this issue comes in the form of painful austerity measures, which inevitably leads to persistent wage and price deflation. Such strict reforms seem hardly enforceable in democratic states for a long duration of time. Adoption of such policies may lead to dangerous destabilization of the political situation in the countries concerned, which would

[26] Available at: http://www.cesifo-group.de/de/ifoHome/policy/Haftungspegel.html

have repercussions on the entire continent. The heavy protests in southern Europe and the growth in the popularity of radical parties gives us a forewarning of the imminent developments.

Against this background, future haircuts and further financial assistance to the debt-burdened countries in the eurozone seems inevitable. In the long run, these measures might not be sufficient to save the shattered national economies of Europe from insolvency. The frequency of transfers from rich nations in favor of the low-growth EMU members is likely to keep on increasing. A large portion of the resulting expense would fall on the shoulders of taxpayers in Germany. The situation gets even worse for German taxpayers if large countries of the euro zone such as Italy or Spain find themselves in serious trouble and asks for assistance. In this case the cost for Germany would be inconceivably huge.

Obviously, an exit from the EMU involves significant costs and would not come free of charge for Germany. As stated earlier, the new German currency would appreciate against the euro and the national currencies of many other countries. According to the calculations of British economist Roger Bootle, German creditors would incur losses amounting to around 160 billion euros, should the new Deutschmark appreciate by 20 percent.[27] This corresponds to seven percent of GDP. The aforementioned figure is undeniably high, but much lower compared to the liability risk that Germany faces with the continuation of the euro rescue mission.

Additionally, capital inflows, which Germany should expect after the re-introduction of the DM, would bring a positive effect as the strong demand for DM would keep German interest rates low in the long run. This would reduce the cost of loans, boosting consumption and investment, thus promoting economic growth. Moreover, appreciation of the new DM would also reduce the debt burden of private and public borrowers.

If Germany were to leave the EMU, costs of currency exchange in commercial transactions with today's euro area countries would arise. Besides, the exchange rate risks would have to be hedged again in the future. The elimination of these charges brought about by the

[27] See *Back to Deutschmark?*, European Alliance for Freedom, p. 20

introduction of the euro remains one of its strongest points. However, the exact amount of this savings is debatable.

Furthermore, one-time charges would also arise from the changes necessary in ATMs, cash registers, and computer software due to the shift from euro to the DM. However, measured in comparison to the three-digit billions required for the rescue of the euro, these amounts seem modest.

5.4 Benefits of the Euro to Germany

The general perception outside Germany is that the nation has been the main beneficiary of the euro and a collapse of the euro would hurt Germany significantly. The argument goes on that had Germany not been a member of the euro, its exchange rate would have been much stronger, and hence its growth lower and unemployment rate much higher than it has been since the beginning of EMU. The mainstream view is that continued upward pressure on the exchange rate of the new German currency would hurt the German economy in the foreseeable future. A study by McKinsey & Company,[28] issued at the beginning of 2012, attempted to substantiate this view. McKinsey estimated that EMU, between its inception and 2010, generated benefits of EUR 330 billion, equivalent to 3.6 per cent of GDP, for its members. The main beneficiary was Germany with a gain of EUR 165 billion or 6.6 per cent of GDP. For France, gains were estimated at only 0.7 per cent of GDP. The first source of benefits (dubbed 'technical') was cost saving from a reduction of transaction and hedging costs. The second ('trade') was a rough estimate of the effects of gains from intensification of intra-EMU trade, through specialization. The third source ('competitiveness') focused on increased economic efficiency. The fourth and last source of benefits ('interest rates') arose from a generally lower level of capital market rates. For EMU as a whole, the biggest gains, according to the study, came from the GDP effects of more intra-EMU trade and lower interest rates.

However, Mayer (2012) argues that it is too simplistic to declare Germany as the outright winner in the competition, when it comes to gaining from the euro. A fallacious assumption

[28] See McKinsey, 'The future of the euro', January 2012

about Germany's benefits from the euro is that a weak currency is a good thing. A weak currency implies feeble terms of trade and hence a modest level of economic welfare. To put it in a simpler way, when the exchange rate of a country is weak, the residents have to produce and exchange more of their products against imports than in a situation where the exchange rate is strong. Most governments care mainly for the short term and hence tend to prefer weak exchange rates. In the long term though, a weak rate has a negative impact on new, innovative companies wanting to come up with new products or more efficient production methods. It keeps incumbent companies in business, even if they produce outdated products in inefficient ways, as they can sell these products abroad at a cheaper price. Thus new entrepreneurs have to compete with these existing inefficient companies for capital, labour, and raw materials. In contrast, a strong exchange rate forces companies to constantly upgrade products, technologies and production methods or go out of business, thereby freeing up resources for new companies. As a result, countries with strong exchange rates tend to have more innovative industries using more up-to-date technologies to produce products for which consumers are willing to pay a premium price, as these goods fulfill their demands, in terms of quality.

Lower exchange rates because of EMU membership undoubtedly resulted in benefits for Germany, but not to the large extent that is often portrayed. In fact, the weaker currency only generated gains for existing companies by reducing competitiveness and removing pressure on them to upgrade their products and technologies. Fortunately, German companies continued to innovate and upgrade their technological levels, regardless of the strength of the euro. Since the early 1970s, the German currency has generally appreciated on trend, forcing German companies to raise efficiency. Such bursts of exchange rate appreciation had been painful and there were frequent calls for the central bank to step in and smooth exchange rate developments. However, the Bundesbank rarely heeded such calls, as emphasis was placed on keeping the DM strong. The positive experience with the DM has established a preference for a strong currency in the minds of German voters, giving the government a mandate to take Germany out of EMU, if the euro turns into a soft currency. So an exit from the EMU is certainly plausible in the future and this might eventually turn out to be economically more beneficial for Germany than remaining in the EMU.

Figure 8 | Approximate Gains from EMU (2010, in % of GDP)

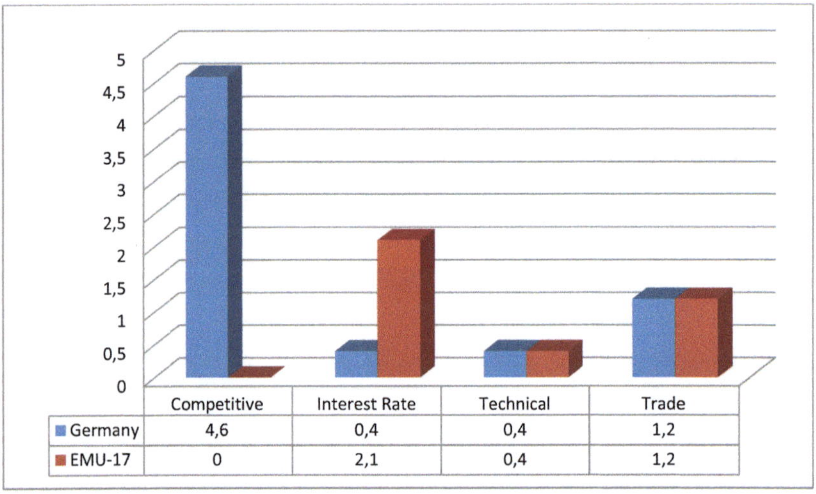

Source: McKinsey, 'The future of the euro', January 2012

If we take a look at the chart above, the most important thing to note here is that approximately 70 percent of the gains from EMU estimated for Germany arrive through an increase in competitiveness. A further 18 percent benefits are associated with an expansion of trade. The remaining gains are attributed in equal parts (6 percent each) to savings in hedging and transaction costs, and interest rates. While the latter can be considered as highly speculative, the former is a direct result of the elimination of exchange rate risk. Mayer (2012) addresses the issue that if the exchange rate had appreciated, the gains from enhanced competitiveness would have been more equally distributed among consumers and companies, instead of only benefiting the latter. Moreover, the gains from increased intra-EMU trade identified in the McKinsey study are actually associated with the build-up of very large current account imbalances, which have led to the balance of payments crisis in EMU. Therefore, we should not count the expansion of imbalanced trade flows as a benefit from EMU.

Since the introduction of the euro, Germany's competitiveness, as measured by the indicator based on unit labor costs provided by the ECB, increased 13.7 percent until 2010. In the same time period, Greece, Spain, Italy and Ireland lost in competitiveness by 11.3, 11.2, 9.4

and 9.1 percent, respectively. Trade surpluses make a currency stronger, while deficits and the resulting foreign debts make a currency vulnerable. Arguably, if Germany still had the Deutschmark, it would have been in an even more superior position by now. After the euro came into existence, German living standards and level of imports did not increase as much as they probably would have with the DM. By contrast, imports remained cheaper for the southern peripheral countries, compared to what the scenario probably would have been without the monetary union. In other words, despite the fact that the peripheral nations lost competitiveness relative to Germany, imports did not increase in price as much as they would have, had these countries relied on their own currencies. Combining this with artificially low interest rates ultimately resulted in the credit-financed consumption boom in the peripheral countries.

From 1999 till 2007, Germany had the second lowest economic growth rate among the major countries in the eurozone. This negative trend was mainly due to the outflow of capital as around two-thirds of German savings or nearly one trillion euros was invested outside Germany during this period. So this money was not available for consumption and investment in the German domestic market. Instead, these German savings were invested mainly in the real estate sector of other EMU countries. Artificially low interest rates due to the introduction of the euro led to a construction boom in the housing markets of countries like Spain, and those funds were diverted there in the hopes of earning higher returns. Therefore, it can be said that Germany has financed to a large extent, both economic growth and the expansion of public and private consumption, particularly in the peripheral countries. These countries of the euro area were thus the actual beneficiaries of the euro, at least in the first few years after the switch to the new currency.

From the perspective of the German economy, the expectation that the monetary union will boost trade in Europe is not applicable any more as Germany's exports to the countries of the eurozone have actually declined in recent years. In 1999, when Germany converted to the single currency, 45.2 percent of all exports went to eurozone countries, but this figure declined to 39.3 percent in 2011.[29] This fall in the level of exports is attributed to the economic weakness of the southern EMU members who could afford to buy fewer German products due to the crisis. In

[29] See *Back to Deutschmark?*, European Alliance for Freedom, p. 6

contrast, German exports to non-European countries, especially to Asia, have increased rapidly over the years despite the fluctuations in exchange rates. In fact, from 2009 to 2011 the German foreign trade with China has increased by nearly 100 percent. Trade activities with India have also risen by around 40 percent. Moreover, German exports to the southern states of the euro area largely exist only on paper, with no guarantees that the full amount will ever be repaid. Due to their economic weakness, it is unlikely that the crisis-hit countries be in a position to generate the required current account surpluses to pay off their debts to Germany. So, intra-EMU trade benefits do not hold significant value for Germany nowadays.

The people who benefit most from the current scenario are the owners of stocks. Not surprisingly, they are happy with the over-inflated capital markets, as the prices of securities and commodities keeps on rising. The leading German Stock Index (DAX) shows remarkable improvement in its performance since the zenith of the financial crisis. The value has increased by more than 100 percent between March 2009 and the end of 2012. This development is clearly down to the expansionary monetary policy of the ECB and the euro rescue bailout packages. The easy money policy has resulted in a liquidity glut due to historically low interest rates and the purchase of ailing government bonds. The extra money did not flow in the economic cycle, but rather looked for profitable investment opportunities in the capital markets, and ended up there. This is the reason why the prices always seem to reach new highs, despite the economic outlook of a looming recession.

Now, let us consider some DAX values over the years to observe the extent of asset inflation in the stock market. The DAX reached the 8,000-point level for the third time in its history, back in mid-2013. The first time was in the boom year of 2000, before it was repeated again in 2007. Both times, this was followed by a price slump. A good indicator of how expensive stocks are is to look at the so-called P/E ratio. It is a way to see how much higher the stock price is compared to the actual earnings of companies. In 2000, on average, the companies listed on the DAX were valued at more than thirty times their annual profit; the P/E ratio was over 30. In 2007, the valuation was not quite so high, but was well over what is considered the normal DAX P/E ratio of 14 to 15 (when seen from a historic perspective). Currently (2016), the average P/E ratio is hovering around 20, once again providing us with ample proof that we are heading towards another slump. Not only that, if we take a look at Figure 9, the DAX astoundingly went beyond the 12,000-point level, recording a peak of 12,374.73 on April 10, 2015. Even though it has come down to the 10,000 mark in 2016, still it represents a highly inflated stock market valuation that gives us sufficient cause for concern.

Figure 9 | DAX (2010 – 2015)

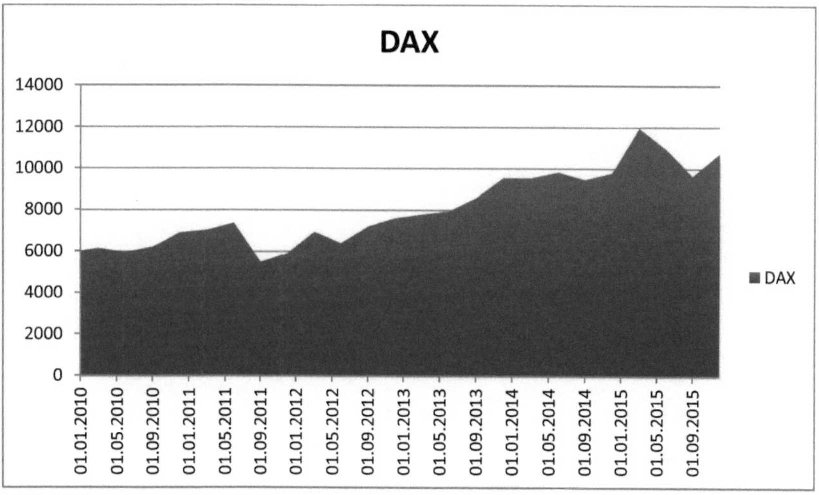

Source: Bloomberg

Anyway, the bottom line is that only the savings of hedging and transaction costs, amounting to an estimated 10 billion euros per year can be safely classified as the true benefits for Germany from EMU. This represents only 6 percent of overall gains (0.4 percent of GDP), which is modest at best. It is difficult to identify any other significant economic benefits of Germany from EMU. The actual benefits from EMU are indeed more political, rather than economic. It may be politically correct to claim that Germany reaps large economic gains from the euro, but it is not all that convincing from an economic viewpoint.

The fact that the German government gave its backing to the Bundesbank's unconditional rejection of any lending by the central bank to governments was probably influenced by the national distress caused by hyperinflation in 1923, which made such operations highly suspicious in the eyes of the electorate. Keeping in mind their historical experience with the debasement of money in the early 1920s, German citizens are very sensitive when it comes to the stability of money (as discussed earlier). So naturally, anything that could be seen as endangering the value of money is frowned upon. Therefore, the ECB's decision to buy government bonds in the secondary market undermined trust in the central bank. Brown (2012) argues that if Germans had been spared the eventual tax burdens of bailing out German banks, along with the re-capitalization of an insolvent ECB, and if their savings had flowed to a much greater extent into a rational investment of foreign assets, they would probably have become the most prosperous nation in the world by now. All in all, it must be said that any new architecture designed for EMU that does not give markets a pivotal role in enforcing economic and fiscal policy discipline, would not be seen as credible.

So, it is now safe to conclude that the euro is a soft currency and definitely nowhere near as strong as the DM used to be. Unfortunately, with the abolition of the DM, not only Germany, but the whole of Europe has lost their anchor of stability. From the perspective of Germany, the continued weakness of the euro currency is the most important reason to consider quitting the monetary union. Furthermore, the argument that a return to the DM would place Germany's exports in jeopardy and plunge the economy into recession should be taken with a grain of salt. Throughout its history, the DM has appreciated frequently, but Germany still managed to increase its foreign sales on a consistent basis. There is no economic reason why this should be any different, once the currency is reintroduced. It is also worthwhile to note that a strong economy needs a strong currency to continually innovate and maintain its competitive advantage. Hence, from a German perspective, it is imperative to consider reverting to the DM.

5.5 Gold-backed DM and Countering Capital Inflows

According to Eichengreen (2011), a currency becomes attractive when the country issuing it is powerful, rich, growing and secure. Needless to say, the economic health of the country issuing the currency is critical for its acquisition and retention of an international role. So the Deutschmark would fulfill the pre-requisites for a strong and stable currency. The DM could even become pegged to gold, which would be the best case scenario in a world riddled with fiat currencies. Rickards (2011) points out that this will redirect resources and creativity toward enhanced technology, productivity improvements and other innovations. Most importantly, growth would be fueled by the creation of real rather than paper wealth.

In terms of backing the currency with gold, it has become obvious now that countries like Germany no longer have a compelling reason to keep their gold in New York or London. Rickards (2014) gives a full account of Germany's gold stock and the future repatriation plans of the Bundesbank by stating that:

> *Germany holds 3,391 tonnes of official gold and is currently the world's second-largest holder after the United States. At the end of 2012, German gold was located as follows: 1,051 tonnes in Frankfurt; 1,526 tonnes in New York; 441 tonnes in London; and 374 tonnes in Paris. On January 16, 2013, the Deutsche Bundesbank, the central bank of Germany, announced an eight-year plan to repatriate all the gold in Paris and 300 tonnes of the gold in New York back to Frankfurt. The gold in London would be left in place, and at the end of the repatriation plan in December 2020, German gold would be 50 percent in Frankfurt, 37 percent in New York, and 13 percent in London.*

Figure 10 | Official Gold Reserves (in Tonnes)

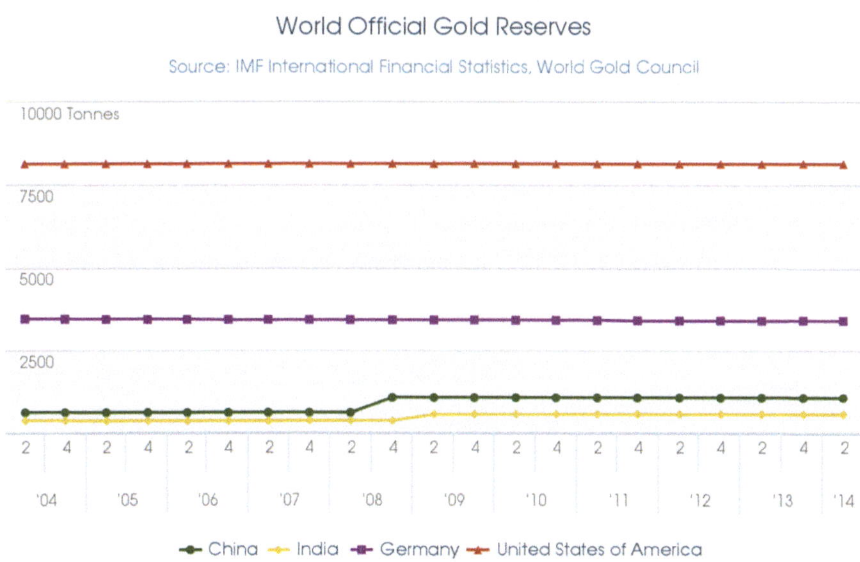

So, there is a clear indication that Germany is seriously considering bringing back its gold reserves, and pegging the new DM to gold may turn out to be a viable option in the not too distant future. Rickards (2014) also suggests that having a gold backed currency is the ideal thing to do for those countries that are inclined to create wealth through skill and entrepreneurship. On the other hand, it is disfavored by those who do not create wealth but instead seek to extract wealth from others through inflation and market manipulation. Moreover, Schiff & Downes (2009) adds that to reassure confidence, it is essential to have adequate gold backing for national currencies. Since gold is a highly valuable commodity, backing a currency by gold will help to restore credibility and preserve the public's faith in that currency.

In the event that Germany reverts to a gold-backed DM, it will have to contend with the issue of high capital inflows, something that is associated with all strong currencies. The Bundesbank has had to deal with such situations before, so it would not be anything new. In the past, whenever the Bundesbank tightened monetary policy with the aim of curbing inflation, its higher interest rates attracted capital from abroad, loosening credit conditions and reigniting inflation fears. Therefore, in order to limit inflows, Germany had to maintain strict restrictions on purchases of money market instruments by nonresidents. Prior approval from the German authorities for sales of domestic fixed-income securities to nonresidents was made a formal requirement, since the early 1970s. In addition, Germany also banned the payment of interest on foreign bank deposits. They raised reserve requirements on foreign-owned bank deposits to discourage capital inflows. By adopting such policies to keep inflation in check, Germany made it clear that it would do whatever is necessary to discourage central banks and governments from accumulating Deutschmarks. In fact, the share of foreign exchange reserves in DM hovered below 15 percent throughout the 1980s.[30] Implementing the aforementioned policies again would be enough to keep the problem of capital inflows under control, once Germany reverts to the DM.

[30] See Eichengreen, 2011, p. 67

Chapter 6: Discussion

Money and Savings

When it comes to a discussion regarding money and central banking, Nobel laureate F.A. Hayek's view that "money is certainly too dangerous an instrument to leave to the fortuitous expediency of politicians" is definitely applicable today. (Hayek, 1976)

When a person saves money, it represents the hours of her life that she spent earning the money, so when that money is destroyed, the time she spent earning it also becomes valueless. So, instead of focusing on borrowing and consumption, the best path to growth would be to increase the amount of savings and trade. Governments pursue a policy of discouraging saving and stimulating spending which they consider to be a way of promoting economic activity, but that is actually the opposite of what would be conducive to real recovery. Consumers who are spending less today are doing the right thing, as this means that they are accumulating savings that will eventually provide the capital investment which entrepreneurs need to create jobs. It will also promote more lending by banks in the future. According to Schiff & Downes (2009), saving instead of borrowing to consume, benefits society in numerous ways; first and foremost, it can finance more capital formation, leading to greater prosperity. Saving money at the present time relieves consumers of burdensome interest payments and also reduces the cost of buying goods. When consumers save over a period of time to make large purchases, they earn accumulated interest, which reduces the cost of purchasing commodities. In contrast, borrowing to make the same purchases increases the total cost by the amount of interest required to be paid. Consumption by means of incurring debt ends up reducing future consumption, as borrowers have to make interest and principal repayments with money they would otherwise be free to spend. So, future consumption can only be enhanced if consumers decide to save more money today.

However, Keynesians consider increased spending as the critical element to promote economic growth, so they view savings as detrimental to growth because the act removes money from circulation and reduces spending. Schiff (2010) raises an important question to counter this view by asking that since everything produced will have to be eventually consumed, why does spending really matter? Even things that no one really wants right now will be consumed if the price falls far enough. People fail to recognize that it is production that adds real value, as nothing can be consumed until it is produced. Saving creates the capital necessary for the expansion of production. Hence, in reality, money saved today makes more of a positive economic contribution than money spent. Unfortunately, the Keynesian system prevalent today has done its best to sever the link between savings and investment. Bearing in mind the current economic conditions persisting worldwide, it is safe to say that Keynes's theory is not the right policy to adopt, if we want to bring ourselves out of the quagmire.

The Austrian School and ABCT

For economists who think that the Austrian School has nothing to add to mainstream economics, it is high time for them to pause and reflect on the Austrian business cycle theory (ABCT). Since mainstream economists have got the cause of the financial crisis and solution to it completely wrong, we should turn to the Austrian economists for answers, since they have got their predictions on-target regarding such matters. The fact that the system has held together for longer than many Austrian economists expected simply means that the financial bubble, the debt, international imbalances and the malinvestments has grown that much bigger that we are on the verge of reaching the point of no return.

Years of market manipulations mean that it would be very difficult (if not impossible) to tighten monetary policy around the world, without facing grave consequences. Raising interest rates might resurrect the collapse in asset values, while further monetary easing runs the risk of precipitating a loss of confidence in money. Only structural changes in European economies can break this deadlock and bring about the desired solution.

Liquidation and Recovery

Anders Aslund, a scholar at the Peterson Institute for International Economics in Washington D.C., suggests that when confronted with a severe economic downturn, an affected nation must try to turn it into a political advantage by acknowledging the crisis, instead of denying its existence. Political leaders who needs to implement tough policies and manages to explain clearly the hard economic choices to the electorate is likely to gain support for those policies, while politicians who deny the depth of the problem will find that the sense of urgency recedes over time and that citizens are less willing to make the necessary sacrifices. This problem is particularly prevalent in the southern European countries. Aslund also urges that countries facing economic crises should elect new leaders with new ideas (Rickards, 2014). It is essential to find leaders who have the courage to be honest with the electorate, and voters who have the strength to accept the hard work required for economic revival. As former Bundesbank president, Karl Blessing, said in a speech delivered in 1966, "there can be no hard currency without hard measures" (Marsh, 1992). Old leadership tends to persist with failed economic policies due to vested interests, while new leaders are able to pursue the cuts in government spending needed to restore fiscal health. Aslund further recommends that the emergency economic responses should be clearly communicated, with more emphasis being placed on spending cuts than tax increases. Citizens will understand and support policies that are explained properly to them but will be reluctant about the need for spending cuts if politicians try to sugarcoat the situation. "Agenda 2010" implemented by Germany years ago (see page 64 for details) can be a good practical example of Aslund's theory, which other countries should try to follow.

If banks had been allowed to fail and no bailout packages were handed out, the year 2011 would have resembled the depression of early 1920s in terms of severity with skyrocketing unemployment and widespread bankruptcies. However, an inflection point would have been reached. Banks would have once again started off from scratch with clean balance sheets and shown a new willingness to lend prudently. Rickards (2014) suggests that private investors would then have found productive assets at bargain prices and started investing. Similarly, the availability of abundant labor (with lower unit labor costs), could have been mobilized to expand productivity, resulting in the commencement of a robust recovery, rather than a lifeless one. The depression would have been over within a year. Instead of taking that severe but less long-lasting hit, the policy makers have prolonged it so much that now we are heading for a far worse disaster.

The depression of 1920-1921 (which is often overlooked) can act as a very instructive case study to demonstrate the above scenario. During and after World War I, the Federal Reserve had been inflating the money supply substantially, and when it finally began raising the discount rate (the rate at which it lends to banks) the economy slowed down considerably, as it began its readjustment in line with ABCT. Woods (2009) observes that the downturn became severe by the middle of 1920 as production fell by an astounding 21 percent, over the following twelve months. However, unlike the Great Depression of the 1930s, it was short lived. This is because the free market was allowed to make the necessary corrections, instead of government meddling in the economy. Even Keynesian economist, Robert A. Gordon admitted that "*government policy to moderate the depression and speed recovery was minimal. The Federal Reserve authorities were largely passive.... Despite the absence of a stimulative government policy, however, recovery was not delayed.*"[31] In a similar vein, economist Benjamin Anderson maintains that: "*The rally in business production and employment that started in August 1921 was soundly based on a drastic cleaning up of credit weakness, a drastic reduction in the costs of production, and on the free play of private enterprise. It was not based on governmental policy designed to make business good*" (Anderson, 1979). The government at that time did not adopt the Keynesian policy of running unbalanced budgets and pumping the printing press to increase expenditures. Instead, the government wisely tried to restrict spending, lower taxes and reduce the public debt.

By contrast, unsurprisingly, the stock market was buoyant before the Great Depression struck. This fact makes perfect sense in light of the Austrian theory. According to ABCT, an inflationary boom will trigger an artificial stimulus to capital-goods industries. Since the value of a company's stock represents the value of the company's capital, a stock market bubble developed, and the subsequent Wall Street crash brought with it immense misery and lasted for a significantly longer period, compared to the previously mentioned depression of 1920-21. In the early 1930s, Robbins correctly observed:

> *"Nobody wishes for bankruptcies. Nobody likes liquidation as such. If bankruptcy and liquidation can be avoided by sound financing nobody would be against such measures. All that is contended is that when the extent of malinvestment and overindebtedness has passed a certain limit, measures which postpone liquidation only tend to make matters worse."* [32]

[31] Robert Aaron Gordon, *Economic Stability and Growth: The American Record* (New York: Harper and Row, 1974), 21-22, cited in Salerno, "An Austrian Taxonomy of Deflation," 95-96.
[32] See Robbins, *The Great Depression*, p. 75.

It cannot be denied that there would have been a severe depression in 2011, but that would have prompted the structural adjustments needed in the European economies. It would also have diverted assets from banking instruments, stocks and bonds toward productive investments in technology and manufacturing. Carlo Bastasin (2012) highlights that German citizens have already experienced first-hand that structural reforms, which increased productivity, were more than proportionally rewarded by increased exports. The resulting growth enhanced government revenues and reduced unemployment. This led to the creation of a virtuous circle, whereby the positive attitude of citizens toward structural reforms encouraged more productivity enhancements by German firms and generated more income for everybody. Moreover, normalized interest rates would have rewarded savers and helped strengthen the euro, resulting in hot money inflows from other regions. Sadly, the policy of kicking the can down the road was adopted, thereby ensuring that none of the aforementioned things materialized in European economies.

Government Deficits and Fiscal Union

Moving on to the issue of deficits and debts, chronic budget deficits have frequently been the precursor for crises. Recent experiences have shown that the longer a government runs deficits, the more its debt level grows and interest payments mount. These payments lay claim to a significant portion of available tax revenues. In addition, there is always the risk that investors may one day conclude that the debt is unsustainable, and start selling bonds en masse resulting in the collapse of the currency on the foreign exchange market. The ECB may once again step into the breach, buying up bonds to support the market just like it bought bonds in May 2010 when panic threatened to engulf European bond markets. However, investors will see this as a never-ending process going round and round in circles. They will interpret the ECB's bond purchases and the pumping of money into the economy as signs of imminent inflation, which will further weaken the euro. Eichengreen (2011) rightly states that the depreciation of euro will feed on itself and there could be mass migration away from the euro, as has happened before.

One scenario that is thought of as having the potential to save the euro is the formation of a fiscal union, but given the sovereignty issues among European nations, that is unlikely to happen. In any case, according to Olivier Blanchard, the former chief economist of the International Monetary Fund (IMF), formation of a fiscal union by pooling common funds, among other things, would still not make the euro function smoothly. He adds that any mechanism to transfer funds from strong to weak nations would only mask the fundamental competitiveness problems that struggling member states must deal with. Fiscal transfers may help a country to get out of a tight spot, but it will also decrease the urge to make the necessary competitiveness adjustment.[33]

Expansionary Monetary Policy

Let us now review the impact easy money policy has on an economy. When the ECB lowers interest rates below the natural level, it has the effect of expanding investment beyond a sustainable level. Based on the wrong signals businesses get from this artificially lowered interest rate, they begin investing as if consumers had the savings to back up the investment. In reality though, real resources are not available, as such a means of lowering the rate of interest does not create new capital. So there is no new wealth available for making good investments. The ECB's policy of artificially lowering rates simply induces investors, borrowers and consumers to misjudge what is going on, leading to resources being misallocated. Market forces set the interest rate at a particular level for a reason, so when central banks tamper with it, they mislead investors into destructive investments that make no sense in the long run. It is the interference with the free market and the refusal to allow market forces to coordinate production and consumption that constitutes the root cause of the problems we face today. Classical economists have taught us that there is no ideal supply of money in a society. The important thing is to ensure that the quality of the money is sound. Prices adjust based on the current money supply. New influx of money into society bestows no social benefit. If production increases and the money supply remain stable, the purchasing power of the money will rise.

[33] See Mehreen Khan, "Fiscal Union will never fix a dysfunctional eurozone, warns ex-IMF chief Blanchard," *The Telegraph*, October 10, 2015.

Similarly, if production falls while the supply of money remains stable, the purchasing power of money will decline. Unfortunately, despite the obvious negative aspects associated with an expansionary monetary policy, the EU money supply keeps on increasing without any sort of restraint, as is depicted in the chart below:

Figure 11 | EU Money Supply: M3

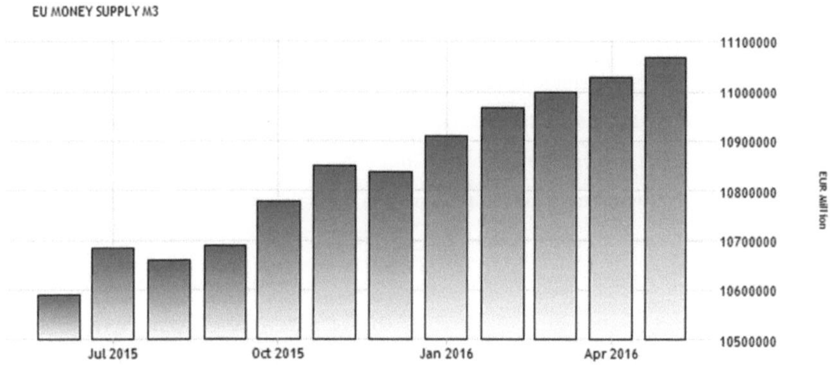

Source: ECB, Tradingeconomics.com

Moral Hazard

If the ECB becomes more interventionist and tries to take up all the private sector debt that builds up, then it will exacerbate the problem of moral hazard, where over the course of the next business cycle, people will once again make bad bets without having to face any negative repercussions. This happens as a result of them having the guarantee of getting bailed out by the government, if things go wrong. Hammond (2012) emphasizes that once the precedent has been established, financial institutions will carry on engaging in riskier investment schemes because they are fully aware that their overextended investment position threatens the stability of the financial system, and will ultimately result in governments purchasing worthless, illiquid assets to bail them out. If we consider the current policies adopted by the major central banks of the world, it becomes apparent that they are the ultimate promoter of consumerism and living only for the present. This brings about a bad dose of cultural distortion where short-term thinking gets the upper hand over long-term planning. Unfortunately, many people who have a concrete understanding of how the monetary system actually operates nowadays are not vocal enough for the general public to find out how it serves the interest of governments and big banks.

Inflation and Deflation

Government and central bank manipulations also give rise to monetary inflation. The main factor that determines whether or not monetary inflation will cause consumer price inflation or asset price inflation is simply what the early receivers of newly created money decide to do with them. They have three choices to choose from: to hold on to the money; to buy financial assets; or use the money for consumption. If they select the first option, naturally, no prices will increase, but we will see asset price inflation, if they choose the second. Deciding to use the money for consumption will result in a rise in consumer prices. Based on what we have seen thus far, most early receivers have clearly decided on buying stocks and other financial assets, thereby overly inflating asset prices.[34]

We have already discussed how inflated the DAX index has become in recent years (see pages 77-78). Now, let us consider NASDAQ, which has also seen an upward trend lately, hitting the threshold of 5,000 after a gap of 15 years in 2015. The previous benchmark was set at the height of the dotcom bubble at 5,132 points in March, 2000. That peak has since been surpassed with NASDAQ recording its highest value of 5,218.859 on July 20, 2015. However, NASDAQ is still not overly inflated at the moment when P/E ratios are taken into consideration, but things are certainly heading towards the danger zone. When the New York Stock Exchange closed on October 9, 2007, the Dow Jones Industrial Average stood at 14,164.53, which was the highest close ever (Woods, 2009). This value was surpassed in early 2013, and since then the valuation has kept on increasing, so much so that it has now gone well past the 18,000 mark (18,472.79 on July 25, 2016). This makes it abundantly clear that investors are dipping their toes into the share market even more nowadays. Central banks are pumping liquidity into the market, but this money rarely reaches the companies. Instead, the majority of the capital is hoarded or

[34] See Karlsson, S., *"Asset Price Inflation and Consumer Price Inflation"*, May 20, 2013. Available at: http://stefanmikarlsson.blogspot.de/2013/05/asset-price-inflation-consumer-price.html

invested in assets such as shares or property, and the excess liquidity drives the rates in the share market upwards. The following charts illustrate this upward trend in NASDAQ and Dow Jones:

Figure 12 | NASDAQ (2010 – 2015)

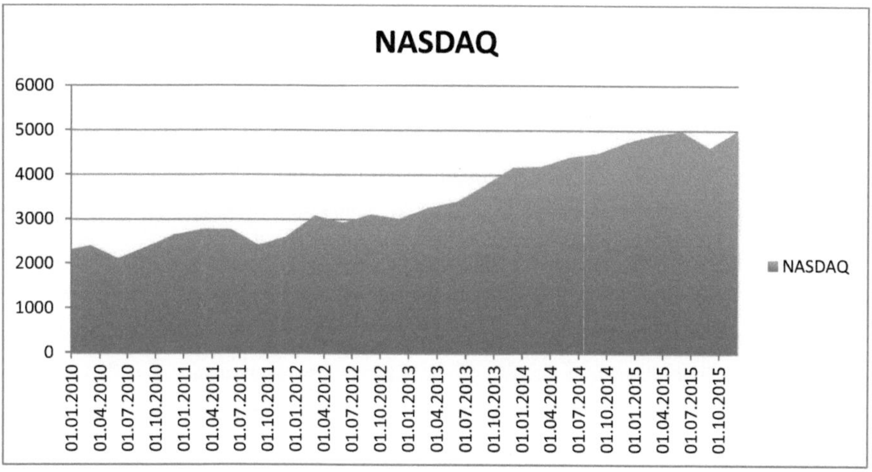

Source: Bloomberg

Figure 13 | Dow Jones (2010 – 2015)

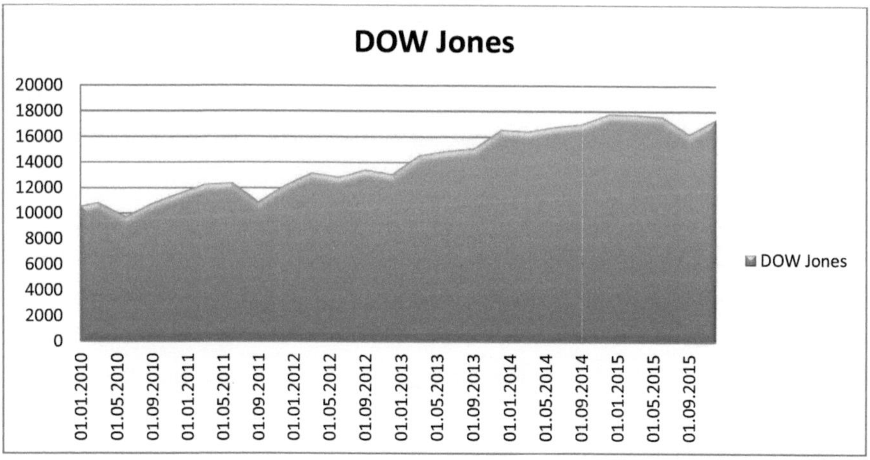

Source: Bloomberg

Rickards (2014) also highlights the concept of money illusion, which dictates that money printing on its own cannot create real growth, but can form an illusion of growth by increasing nominal prices and nominal GDP. This illusion cannot last forever though and will be eventually shattered, but it can persist for a decade or more before inflation emerges with a lag and steals the superficial gains. This is the phase we are going through right now.

When price eventually rises, it represents a devaluation of the euro and acts as a tax on the general population. This tax hits the middle class and poor people the hardest, while rich people are let off the hook. As discussed earlier, this is because the early users of the money, comprising of governments, banks, and big corporations are the real beneficiaries of monetary inflation. Now let us imagine a situation where firms or banks connected to the government receive a new injection of money, courtesy of Fed credit expansion. This money is created out of thin air, and does not come from the sale of some goods previously manufactured. Therefore, when these institutions spend the money, they are in effect taking goods out of the economy without providing anything in return themselves. This clearly demonstrates how they benefit at the expense of the rest of society (Woods, 2009).

Another case in point is that if an increased abundance of goods keeps pushing prices lower, a higher money supply, by putting upward pressure on prices, could cancel out that downward trend and keep the overall price level stable. This would mean that most people would not notice a rise in the price level, but nevertheless, inflation in terms of an increased money supply has certainly taken place. In such a case, the inflation deprives people of the rise in living standards that would have materialized from falling prices.

Even if consumer prices does not rise immediately, it can show up in asset prices, leading to bubbles in stocks, commodities, and other hard assets, something which is noticeable again today. Recent events like the tech stock crash in 2000 or the housing bubble in 2007 clearly illustrates how such bubbles are susceptible to bursting sooner rather than later. Due to the fact that high levels of government-induced inflation has not yet led to big rises in the baskets of consumer goods used in official price calculations, politicians and their Keynesian-influenced economists continually boast about low inflation rates. On this issue, Rothbard (1963) states: "The fact that general prices were more or less stable during the 1920s told most economists that there was no inflationary threat, and therefore the events of the great depression caught them completely unaware." So, we may well be witnessing a case of history repeating itself here.

The Keynesians also conveniently tend to ignore the fact that the expansion of money and credit progressed at a faster rate than economic growth. Sharp rises in other asset prices, like stocks and real estate are simply not captured in the consumer price baskets. These price increases ensure that the relatively small group of asset holders becomes richer, while those depending on fixed incomes or earning low wages lose out.

Moreover, inflation allows governments to cunningly avoid making difficult decisions and artificially reduce the level of debt. By means of printing money, governments can nominally pay back the money they owe, but they do so by diluting their currency. Creditors get paid, but what they receive is not worth as much as the value the money had when it was lent out. Schiff (2010) adds to the discussion by suggesting that during a recession, prices need to fall in order to rebalance the economy. Recessions should be deflationary to a certain extent, as falling prices will help to cushion the blow of low employment. Somehow, most modern economists blame falling prices for demand destruction. They fail to consider the fact that when prices fall far enough, people automatically start spending again. This process enables prices to fall to a level justified by underlying supply and demand conditions, and unwanted inventories to be chalked off. By keeping prices artificially higher, the aforementioned process never takes place. Rickards (2014) explains further that deflation is endogenous, which is derived from emerging markets' productivity, balance sheet deleveraging, and demographic shifts. On the other hand, inflation is exogenous, resulting from interest rate manipulations and easy money policy of central banks. In a nutshell, governments want to inflate while the world wants to deflate. Rickards writes:

> *"Neither force will relent, so the pressure between them will continue to build. It is just a matter of time before the economy experiences more than just bubbles, but an earthquake in the form of either a deeper depression or higher inflation, as one force rapidly and unexpectedly overwhelms the other."*

Deflation is often misunderstood as having adverse effects on an economy when in actual fact falling prices merely lead to redistribution. Buyers win at the expense of sellers, but these sellers are also buyers, so the impact can cancel each other out. Similarly, debtors lose out in the case of price deflation, but it allows the creditors to gain. If a company goes bankrupt, the creditor takes over the assets and may continue production if the business only went under due to its debt, but is otherwise in a workable condition. This change in ownership does not make factories and machinery disappear, so the productive potential of the economy is not disturbed. Thus, price deflation only leads to redistribution and is not as big of an economic problem as it is generally made out to be.[35]

If central banks had instead allowed deflation to take place as the economic conditions dictated, real incomes would have risen even without nominal gains, because prices of consumer goods would have been lower. Thus, deflation would have enhanced the standard of living even when wages remained stagnant. In a way, deflation of money stock is actually the beginning of the process of economic healing. Deflation helps to stop the transfer of wealth from genuine wealth producers to various nonproductive bubble activities. Deflation shatters the illusion of prosperity created by monetary inflation. Contrary to mainstream thinking, deflation removes various bubble activities thereby strengthening the process of wealth generation.[36] So, it is totally understandable that those who benefit from inflation are exaggerating the potential negative effects of deflation.

We should acknowledge that there is enough uncertainty already prevalent in entrepreneurship, even without adding inflation and deflation to the list of barriers standing in the way of innovation. It is important for policy makers to finally realize that the more drama that they can remove from central banking, the more certainty will be provided to entrepreneurs, who are the real source of jobs and wealth creation.

Another important point to emphasize as part of the discussion is that job creation comes largely from small businesses, and not courtesy of big businesses. So when the ECB distorts the

[35] See Philipp Bagus, "In Defense of Deflation: A Conversation with Philipp Bagus," *The Austrian* 2, no. 2 (March-April 2016): 15–17.

[36] See Frank Shostak, *"Central Bankers are Wrong About Inflation and Deflation"*, Mises Wire, June 14, 2016. Available at: https://mises.org/blog/central-bankers-are-wrong-about-inflation-and-deflation

interbank lending market by keeping interest rates too low, it deprives small businesses of working capital loans and hurts their ability to create new jobs. This begs the question: Why is the ECB so fearful of deflation that it resorts to extraordinary policy measures designed to cause inflation? The ECB prefers inflation because it reduces the debt-to-GDP ratio, erases government debt, props up the banks, and can be taxed. On the other hand, deflation has an adverse effect on all of the above, but may help consumers and workers, so governments and central banks are firmly against it.

Unemployment

An aspect that often gets lost in the midst of the inflation or deflation debate is that the European Union is still experiencing staggering levels of unemployment. Even though unemployment figures have shown an improving trend in recent years, the fact that the numbers are still high suggests that not enough has been done to address the situation. Currently (as of May, 2016), the EU as a whole has 8.6 percent of the workforce unemployed and 10.1 percent in the eurozone.

Breaking these numbers down to the national levels show just how bad the unemployment levels are in the different member countries. The highest unemployment rate is in Greece, where it is nearly 24.1 percent of the workforce. Spain, is not dealing much better with an unemployment rate that is close to 20 percent; Portugal and Italy are both hovering around the 11.5 percent mark. Among the PIIGs, only Ireland has an unemployment rate (7.8 percent), which is lower than the EU average. France has unemployment that is just under 10 percent; even countries that are considered affluent, like Austria and Sweden, is suffering from unemployment of 6.1 percent and 7 percent, respectively. Out of the 28-member countries of the EU, only Germany, Malta and Czech Republic have unemployment of less than 5 percent. Such readings do not bode well for the EU and eurozone. The chart below gives us the full picture regarding the unemployment situation currently prevailing in EU:

Figure 14 | Unemployment Rates in EU (May, 2016)

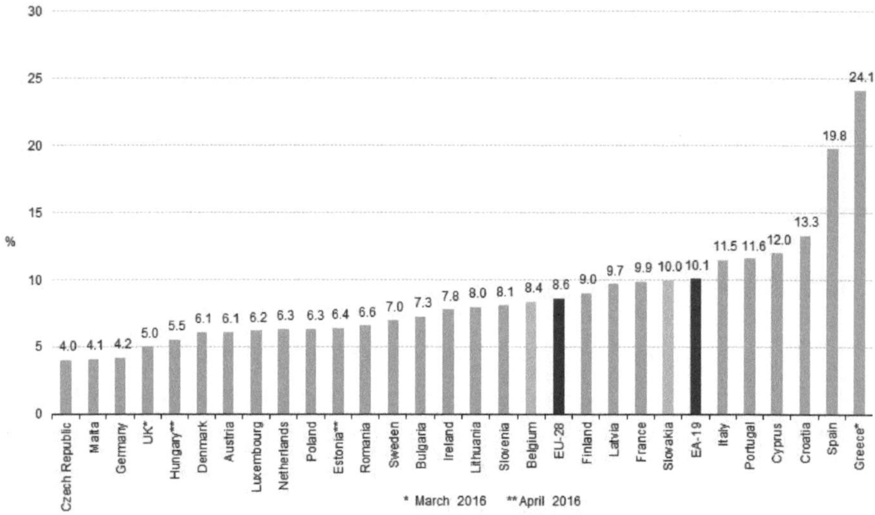

Source: Eurostat

Youth unemployment, which is defined as people between 16 and 25 years of age who are unable to find desired work, paints an even more catastrophic picture. Based on 2015 data (Eurostat), average youth unemployment is over 20.4 percent for the EU as a whole, and more than 22.5 percent in the eurozone. In Greece and Spain, youth unemployment rate is very close to 50 percent; in Italy and Portugal the rate stands at 42.7 percent and 32.6 percent respectively (see Figure 15); it is almost 25 percent in France and over 20 percent in Sweden. Only in Austria and Germany is youth unemployment less than 10 percent. All the other EU countries are in the double-digit range.

Average youth unemployment for the entire eurozone has also not declined to anywhere near a desirable level. The rate stood at 22.5% in 2015, which is lower than the 2013 peak of 24.4%, but significantly higher compared to pre-crisis year of 2007 when the rate was around

15%. In fact, since 2009 the rate has stayed above 20% (see Figure 16 below), thereby giving us yet another indication that current policies are not working.

Figure 15 | Country-Specific Youth Unemployment (March, 2015)

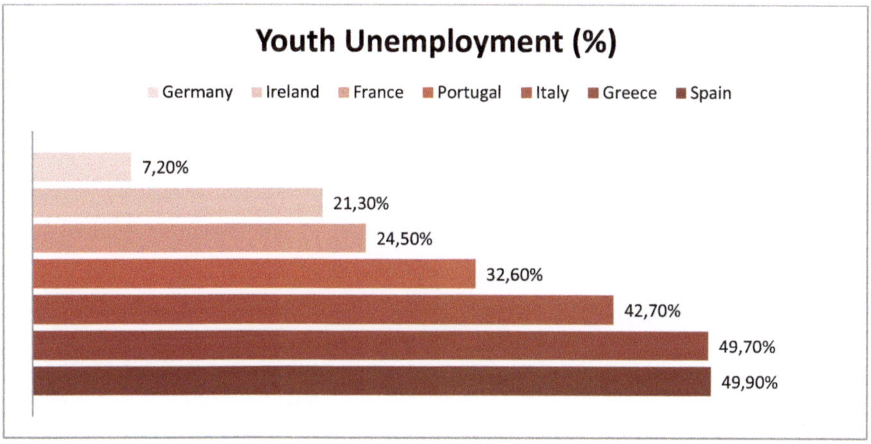

Source: Eurostat, Statista

Figure 16 | Average Youth Unemployment in Eurozone (2007 - 2015)

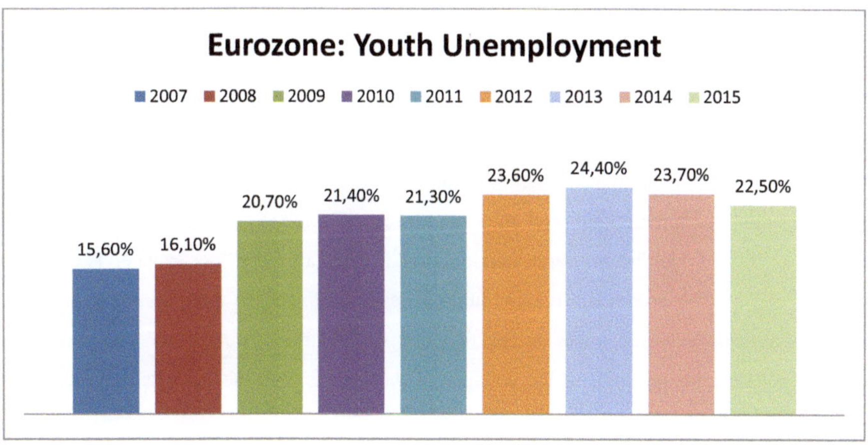

Source: Eurostat, Statista

Economic Models

It is noteworthy that in the late 1940s, economics terminated the association with its former allies in political science, philosophy and law, and sought a new alliance with the hard sciences of applied mathematics and physics. Unfortunately, we find no evidence to suggest that it has had any success in mitigating the classic problems of boom and bust. In fact, there is overwhelming evidence to suggest that the modern practice of economics has left society worse off when one considers the excessive debts (both sovereign and private), government deficit spending, rising inequality in the distribution of income, bouts of inflation, and ever increasing unemployment. Furthermore, Rickards (2014) argues that current financial regulatory policy is misguided because the risk-management models are unsound. The disconcerting issue is that despite knowing that the models are unsound, people still use them because these models permit higher leverage, and more profits and bonuses. The regulators are well-informed about this but prefer to play along, often in the hope of getting a job in the institutions they regulate, clearly bringing into play a conflict of interest.

Recent failures have stripped economists of their immunity from rigorous scrutiny by the general public. Claims by economic theorists about multipliers, correlation and normally distributed risk have become threats to the well-being of the nations worldwide. There have been repeated economic failures in central bank policies and Keynesianism. Understanding these failures will allow us to comprehend why growth has stalled in most major economies, and financial crises looms on the horizon every few years.

Varoufakis (2013) expertly explains how most policy makers nowadays try to get away with making wrong predictions. Whenever they observe an unexpected deviation of human behavior from their predictions, and they are unable to explain it, they simply label such behavior as 'out of equilibrium', and then consider it to be a random occurrence. The models work so long as the 'deviations' remain subdued, and the financiers keep on earning profits. However, as soon as panic arises in the financial system, these 'deviations' turn out to be anything but random, resulting in the collapse of the models, and the markets they helped to create.

Goodhart's Law which was first articulated by Charles Goodhart in a 1975 paper published by the Reserve Bank of Australia can be used to highlight the misdeeds of central banks. Goodhart's Law is frequently paraphrased along the lines, "When a financial indicator becomes the object of policy, it ceases to function as an indicator." That paraphrase captures the essence of Goodhart's Law, but the original formulation, "Any observed statistical regularity will tend to collapse once pressure is placed upon it for control purposes" is even more insightful. This emphasized the point that Goodhart was not only concerned with manipulation or market intervention, but also on a particular kind of top-down effort by central banks to dictate outcomes in complex financial systems. Economic systems cannot approach optimality through policies imposed by central banks. They reach optimal state spontaneously via market forces. Central banks like the ECB and the Fed relies on price signals, particularly those related to inflation, unemployment, stock prices, commodity prices and several other variables. So what happens when price signals from already manipulated markets are used to derive polices? This is essentially the question posed by Goodhart's Law. The answer is simple; it leads to the formulation of far from optimal policies and wrong outcomes.

German Economy and European Periphery

In Germany, a rethinking of monetary policy began in the year 2009, marking a turning point in public attitudes as well. At that time, Thorsten Polleit, the respected chief economist at Barclays Germany, along with Joseph Salerno of the Mises Institute in the United States and Guido Hülsmann of the University of Angers, France, publicly recommended a return to the gold standard, and their recommendation was quoted in the popular German magazine *Der Spiegel*. This ensured a wide German audience for a discussion regarding sound monetary policy. [37]

A notable thing about Germany is that its overall trade surplus is so large that it cannot be seriously impaired by problems in the peripheral countries. Germany's fastest-growing share of trade now comes from non-European markets. Bastasin (2012) highlights that the emerging markets of Brazil, China, India, and Russia, trade with Germany six times more in volume than they do with France, and twenty times more than they do with Spain. The trade balance is driven

[37] See "The Curse of Cheap Money," *Der Spiegel, January 19, 2009.*

mainly by a country's relative competitiveness and the strength of internal demand relative to external demand. A key factor in determining competitiveness is labor costs, which had increased dramatically faster in most other countries, compared to Germany. The competitiveness of peripheral countries can be restored through faster productivity growth or relative wage restraint. However, improving productivity is a lengthy process, which requires a lot of effort and sacrifice. The spending cuts and tax increases imposed as austerity measures on the troubled countries can only be considered as a short-term solution. Long term planning is essential to get these countries out of the quagmire. There was a sizeable loss of international competitiveness in Portugal, Ireland, Italy, Greece and Spain. So, wages have to be forcefully restrained to regain international competitiveness. Since joining a monetary union means giving up the policy lever of currency devaluation, the only option left to restore international competitiveness is an internal devaluation, focused on wages. But wage restraint is a painful process that decreases incomes and hence the burden on consumers and producers, restricting consumption expenditures and investments. It can initially slow down the growth rate, thus making the debt-to-GDP ratio even higher. All these things point to the inherent weakness in the euro, and bring into question the sustainability of the currency itself.

As far as Germany is concerned, most financial experts agree that the easy money policy of the ECB will eventually lead to a rise in prices in the medium term. A suggestion has been put forward that Germany must become economically weaker, so that the crisis-afflicted states of the euro zone can catch up in economic terms. This objective can be achieved by increasing prices of German goods and services, because this would dampen the demand from the foreign countries. At the same time, the sales prospects of exportable goods of the peripheral nations will be enhanced. According to calculations by the Ifo Institute Munich, price inflation in Germany would have to increase for a decade by around 5.5 percent per annum, so the euro crisis economies can make the necessary adjustments without deflationary shock.[38] Whichever way we look at it, this suggestion seems to be a rather preposterous one, as no country should willingly bring high levels of inflation on itself for the benefit of others. Germany can avoid such a scenario by disassociating itself from the euro. This would mean a return to the stable

[38] See *Back to Deutschmark?*, European Alliance for Freedom, p. 8

Deutschmark, and the Bundesbank would once again be able to place its focus on sound money and pursue an independent monetary policy.

For Germany, the re-introduction of the Deutschmark would naturally bring with it substantial costs. However, these costs will be much lower than what politicians and media sources proclaim. In the not-too distant future, German policymakers will have to decide whether to accept the increasing burdens of the euro rescue mission or return to the DM. The decision will have to be made when massive tax increases in Germany will become necessary to finance new haircuts in favor of bankrupt states in southern Europe. Such a case will naturally enlarge negative public opinion further and increase the domestic political pressure on the German government. Then, the re-introduction of the DM would be on the political agenda, even though it may seem illusive today. Back in 2010, in Seoul, German Chancellor Merkel stated clearly her views regarding taxpayers having to bear most of the burden:

> *"Let me put it simply: in this regard there may be a contradiction between the interests of the financial world and the interests of the political world. We cannot keep constantly explaining to our voters and our citizens why the taxpayer should bear the cost of certain risks and not those people who have earned a lot of money from taking those risks."* [39]

Furthermore, if the crisis-afflicted nations refuse to take proper action towards servicing their debts, this would pave the way for Germany to leave the EMU legally. Although the Maastricht Treaty does not include a clause whereby a single member can get out of the EMU, the German Constitutional Court has already delivered the verdict in 1993 that Germany can leave the union, in case of monetary instabilities surfacing within the union. It has to be said that we are on the verge of reaching that stage.

Public Perception of EU

On June 23, 2016, people in the United Kingdom voted on a referendum to determine whether to stay or leave the European Union, which became known as Brexit. The fact that the

[39] See Peter Spiegel and David Oakley, "Irish Contagion Hits Wider Eurozone," *Financial Times*, November 12, 2010.

British people decided to vote in favor of "leave" does not come as much of a surprise based on a pre-referendum survey conducted by Pew Research Center, which found that euro-skepticism is on the rise across Europe. A median of only 51% across ten EU countries surveyed have a favorable view of the union now.[40] The British are not the only ones having doubts about the EU, as in a number of nations the portion of the public with a favorable view of the Brussels-based organization has fallen markedly. Only 27% of the Greeks, 38% of the French and 47% of the Spanish have a favorable view of the EU, while the German are almost evenly split at 50%. EU favorability went down 17% in France between 2015 and 2016; Spain saw a decline of 16%, Germany 8%, the UK 7% and Italy 6% in the same time period. In fact, most of the major EU countries have seen a declining trend in EU favorability, as can be seen on the chart below:

Figure 17 | EU Favorability in Selected Nations (2004 - 2016)

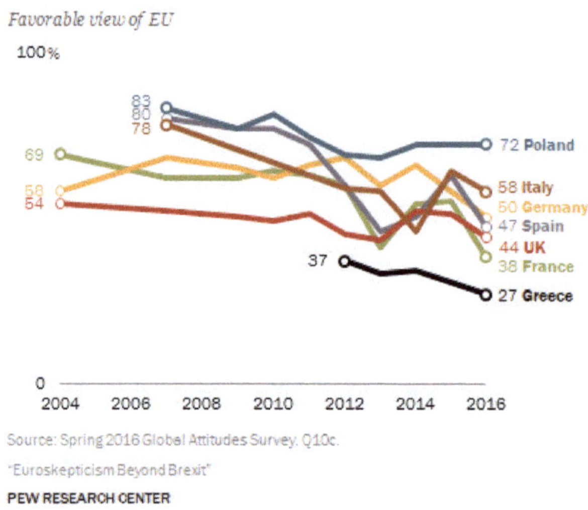

Having observed this negative trend, one must point out that the European Union has its merits and so not all countries should consider leaving the union. Britain voted in favor of leaving EU, but they are likely to face negative consequences because of this. What we need to focus on more critically is approval rating of EU's handling of economic issues, most importantly the currency issue. This is where the main problem of the union resides. As touched

[40] See Pew Research Center, June, 2016, "Euroskepticism Beyond Brexit"

upon earlier, the costs of remaining within the EMU are very high, in the form of bailouts and guarantees for rescue funds. The euro is a misconstruction in the sense that several independent governments can finance their deficits through one central banking system. The incentive is to run higher deficits than other states of the EMU and this setup made interest rates converge, thereby enabling monetary redistribution. Before the inception of the euro, interest rates varied considerably among the European nations, as shown on the chart below:

Figure 18 | Three-month Interest Rates in Germany & PIIGS (1987-1998)

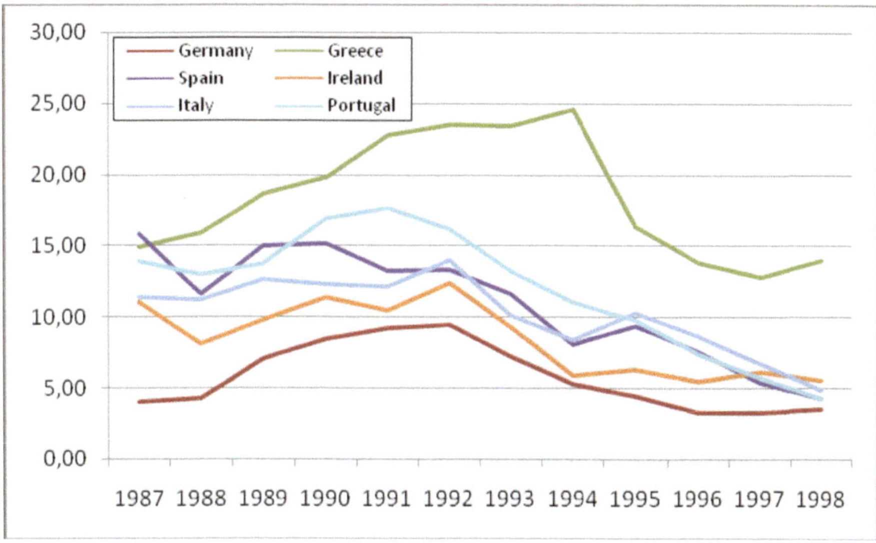

Source: Eurostat

So, for a country like Germany, the best course of action would be to withdraw from the EMU but not the EU itself. Several critics highlight that the Maastricht Treaty does not provide for a mechanism to exit the EMU and hence such a withdrawal would constitute a breach of the Treaties. In an ECB working paper published in 2009, Athanassiou (2009) claims that a country that exits the EMU would have to leave the EU as well. As the Lisbon Treaty allows for secession from the EU, withdrawal from the EU would provide the only way for a country to get rid of the euro. The solution to this legal problem could be a simultaneous exit from both the

EMU and EU, and then reentering EU immediately or after a short lag. The exact process of doing this could be negotiated beforehand. In the case of a big contributor to the EU budget such as Germany, the country should not face many difficulties when it comes to gaining readmission to the EU.[41]

Coming to the approval ratings of economic issues in the EU, one glance at Figure 19 gives us a fairly good idea of how much dissatisfaction currently persists regarding these policies. Disapproval rating is naturally very high in crisis-ridden countries with Greece leading the way, where 92% of the population has a negative view, according to the survey. Even in countries like France and the United Kingdom, disapproval ratings stand at 66% and 55% respectively. Only in Germany more people are still in favor of the economic policies, but that will surely change if the instability continues.

Figure 19 | Approval Rating: Economic Issues (2007 - 2015)

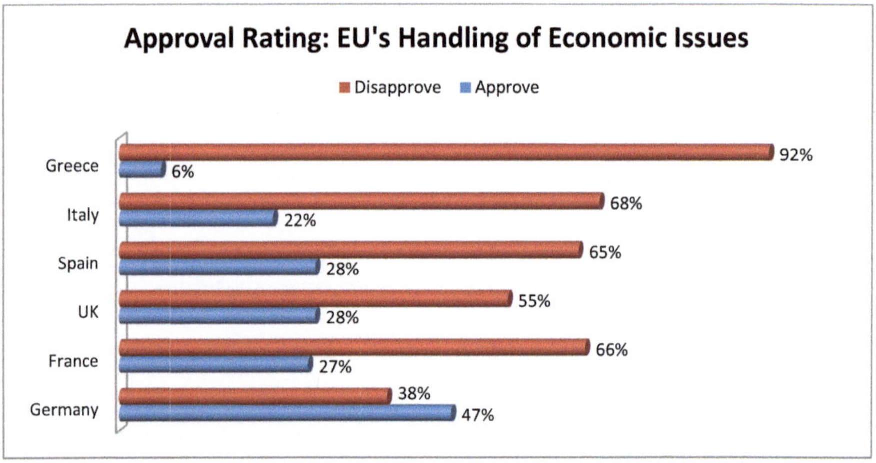

Source: Pew Research Center

[41] See Phillip, Bagus. 2012. "Practical Steps to Withdraw from the Euro." Submission for: The Wolfson Prize.

The Way Forward

Bastasin (2012) suggests that a run on the banks of weaker nations is a possibility that could happen anytime, without prior warning. If such a scenario materializes, the eurozone could be torn apart. Capital would be hastily repatriated, and the European internal market would break into pieces. Widespread poverty would result from defaults, followed by capital controls and protectionism, none of which is a good sign for the future of European prosperity.

So, this brings us to the question of what the future of the eurozone should be like. Should there be a full political and fiscal union? That proposition is desirable, but highly unlikely considering the sovereignty issue. Then, should the policymakers continue to kick the can down the road? Certainly not is the easy answer to that query. As we have discussed thus far, continuing with the current expansionary monetary policy would only make things worse. This leaves us with the option of dismantling the single currency altogether, which we believe would be the best way forward, considering the circumstances.

Additionally, it is of utmost importance that a market-based agenda is put in place for growth and job creation. The following steps provide us with the best way forward:

- A monetary policy aiming for sound money should be implemented with immediate effect, even if abolishing the central bank system is unattainable at present.
- Controlling the supply of money and credit should be left to the market, so that it can determine the correct level of interest rates and provide us with the truth about savings availability and investment profitability for long-run sustainable growth. Monetary expansion sends out false signals which distort the normal functioning of the market economy and hence should be stopped.
- Foster more entrepreneurial spirit by significantly reducing marginal personal tax rates and corporate taxes. This would create greater incentives and provide the financial means for private investment, and creation of jobs.
- Distinguished Professor Dr. Richard Ebeling proposes a reduction in government spending by a minimum of 10 percent more than tax cuts in order to move the European governments in the direction of a balanced budget without any tax increases.

- Eliminate or reduce government regulatory policies over the business sector to allow competitive forces to operate and bring about the required adjustments and corrections for restoring economic balance.

Sadly, until now, the response of policymakers to the crisis has been anything but free market-based. Vogt & Leuschel (2011) emphasizes that prosperity does not develop from manipulations by bureaucrats in the form of experimentations in interest-rate fixing or wealth redistribution. Prosperity is derived from free enterprise, and solving problems through market mechanisms. Only by means of exploring new market-based pathways can we hope to attain a level of prosperity that has never been achieved before.

Chapter 7: Conclusion

Many people may be of the opinion that the economic collapse is over, but the reality is that an even bigger one is looming on the horizon. The events we have witnessed thus far are the catalysts for the catastrophic monetary disaster awaiting Europe in the not-so-distant future.

Unfortunately, most human beings are susceptible to believe in something (regardless of how absurd it is in rational terms), as long as they are part of a group that subscribes to the same mainstream viewpoint. Individuals who otherwise might be rational human-beings are often swept up into irrational groups that force them away from thinking logically and applying common sense in decision-making. This tendency of following the crowd is the root cause of a lot of financial difficulties that we face today. So, it is high time for people to unshackle themselves from such groups. We should all give due consideration to the Austrian School of economic thought as it certainly provides us with a rational approach for the future.

Most mainstream economists believe that demand can be increased by simply giving people more money to spend. However, what they fail to realize is that this does not change real demand, but just increases how much people can spend on items that have already been produced. Expanding the money supply by printing unlimited money, and the ability of governments and corporations to take on huge debts have hidden the fact that real credit is actually limited by a finite supply of savings. People can get more of what they demand only by means of increasing the supply level. Like any other resource, savings must be accumulated before it can be lent out, so it is naïve to think that all it takes for a credit market to function properly is willing borrowers.

Another fallacy of many modern economists is the assumption that spending drives growth, and that when deflation is present, people tend to defer purchases, so as to allow prices to fall even further. They theory goes that when consumers eventually do spend money to make purchases, the diminished price makes less of an economic impact. This is an absurd proposition as consumers do not need to be persuaded when it comes to spending. We know that human wants are unlimited, so if people do not want something there is usually a genuine reason behind it. Either the product is not good enough or it is beyond the reach of the consumers in terms of affordability. In any case, the act of saving instead of spending (or deferring purchases) is made based on rational decisions and tends to benefit the economy as a whole, so it should not be discouraged.

Vogt & Leuschel (2011) claims that the banking crisis of 2008 and the sovereign debt crisis of 2010 are not failures of the market, but rather the consequences of monumental failures in monetary policy, and we could not agree more with this view. Sound money is the foundation of healthy and sustainable economic growth. By contrast, the abuse of the printing press to create money out of thin air leads to the impoverishment of broad sections of the population.

The central banks should be held accountable for price inflation, recession, depression, and excessive debt, which brings into play the boom-bust cycles. Adopting an expansionary monetary policy with the intention of tackling deflation may eventually result in a loss of confidence in the fiat currency system, which will turn out to be the greater of two evils. Once an inflationary mindset grabs hold of the general population, it may prove impossible for central banks to contain or reverse the trend. There is a high risk of losing confidence in the euro if runaway inflation materializes. Rickards (2014) observes that confidence in a monetary system, once lost, can rarely be reinstated. Unfortunately, the ECB does not seem to understand that money creation can be an irreversible process. Abandoning sound money may work for a short period of time, but after a certain point, confidence in money can be lost, requiring an entirely new system to rise in its place.

Moving on to Germany, exiting the EMU would undeniably impose significant losses on German citizens. However, these losses will be much lower than continuing with the euro rescue mission, which entails incalculable risks and costs. If Germany reverts to the hard, stable Deutschmark, the German population would once again have bright monetary prospects for the future. The fear that their wealth will be destroyed by rising inflation caused by expansionary monetary policy pursued to protect the euro will vanish. The end of the euro would not be a calamity, as its proponents claim, but would actually help to bring new opportunities for increasing economic growth in the medium to long-term future.

The DM stood as the symbol for the economic rise of Germany after the Second World War. Sadly, this national symbol was taken away from the Germans without the citizens having a proper say regarding the matter. The single currency was adopted as a political matter, more than anything else. Therefore, it is time for Germany to undo the error and move out of the monetary union (but stay in the EU). If Germany reverts to the DM, a big problem would be unwanted capital inflows from abroad in advance of the changeover: Sensing the availability of a strong and stable currency in a world where sound money is rare, many countries would try to transfer their money to Germany. Although that would bring new capital for investment into the country, it would also bring with it inflation risks. Therefore, the Bundesbank would have to counter this with adequate monetary policy measures to limit the adverse effects on price stability in Germany. The experience during the last era of DM provides ample proof that the German central bank has the necessary expertise and the monetary policy instruments at its disposal to meet this challenge.

The correct approach towards tackling the "too big to fail" issue is to eradicate that concept by breaking up big banks and limiting their activities to deposit taking, provision of loans (both commercial and consumer loans), and a few other useful services. Breaking up big banks would make the costs of failure much more containable, thereby ensuring that it does not threaten the entire financial system. So the solution towards avoiding systemic risk is to break down big banks into smaller units that are not too big to fail. If that is not possible, then as per the Austrian school of economic thought, the banks should be allowed to go bankrupt, with new, more prudent banks taking their place. The fate of Lehman Brothers can be used as a prime example of what happens to a firm and the rest of the economy, when it is allowed to go bankrupt. With approximately 26,000 employees and assets worth $639 billion, Lehman could have made a good case that it was too big to fail. However, as we all know, that did not turn out to be the case. Whatever had value worth preserving in Lehman found its way into the hands of other owners when it went bankrupt in September 2008 (Woods, 2009). What the pundits seem to ignore is that the free market already has clear rules governing bank failures, so there is no need to meddle with it, using systemic risk as an excuse.

In addition, based on the current situation we face today, reintroducing gold into the monetary system should be given serious thought. A 100 percent gold standard (where money is backed fully by gold) may sound like a pipe-dream at the moment, but under this standard, credit expansion is impossible. If banks have to maintain 100 percent reserves on their demand deposits, they simply cannot engage in money printing. Even a fractional reserve gold standard would help to limit credit expansion, and keep it to a manageable level. Moreover, if the world had been on a gold standard, currency mismatching and the dangers associated with it would have been eliminated. A country could not have possibly indebted itself massively in its domestic currency or in mismatching foreign currencies, as both currencies would have been backed by gold. This would have gone a long way towards ensuring the solvency of banks.

Nowadays, people tend to worry about what would happen in a world without central banks. The answer is actually quite simple. Paul (2009) claims that non-existence of central banks would not lead to a decline in modern economic life, but rather it would eliminate bubbles, unsustainable trade imbalances, excessive growth of government debt, and inflation. We are inclined to support this point of view. In the absence of central banks, banking would operate by responding to the wishes of consumers, just like in the case of self-regulating markets. In fact, if we look back at history, from 1836 to 1913, the United States had no central bank, yet it was a period of innovation, high economic growth, and unprecedented prosperity.

As Ludwig von Mises demonstrated in his widely acclaimed book titled *Human Action*, the issue is not just that central planning and interventionism might not work, the reality is that it cannot work. The reason behind this is quite simple. We do not have the ability to predict human action that will take place in the future, so models, forecasts, and other forms of data-crunching does not really hold much value. Every human being acts in their own way, keeping in mind their respective self-.interests. Their individual preferences cannot be determined by anyone else, and the ways in which they will respond to things, events or occurrences cannot possibly be predicted with certainty.

Unfortunately, in the minds of interventionists, spending more money remains the cure for budget deficits. Similarly, the cure for inflation or deflation is to print more money. In other words, it seems like they believe that the way to get out of a deep hole is to increase the rate of digging, and the sad reality is that we are still implementing such outrageous economic policies. So the important question to answer now is whether the ECB will continue to protect the banks or save the euro because it cannot save both. If money is constantly printed in order to support the balance sheet of banks, the value of the euro will inevitably be undermined.

Instead of trying to prop up the European economy by increasing debt, policy makers should allow it to take the hit, so that a stronger economy can be built in its place. Economic collapse has only been postponed, courtesy of bailout packages offered to companies deemed as too big to fail. Refusing to allow market forces to repair the damage will only weaken the structure further, making complete collapse almost inevitable. It is important for us to realize that we need to deal with this mess head-on, instead of prolonging the agony further. Self-regulating market forces would help to bring excess spending under control, replenish depleted savings, liquidate bad investments, fund capital investment, and create more jobs. Unfortunately, the bubble that is currently growing in the stock market threatens to dwarf all preceding asset bubbles. Once this bubble bursts, consumer prices will soar and there will be a devastating effect on the economies of the world. The good news is that if free market forces are allowed to operate unconstrained, the economies can be rebalanced, thereby setting the stage for a real expansion.

As we have so often stated, there is no doubt in our minds that a huge economic disaster is just around the corner. Government manipulation of economies has reached such a stage that it is difficult to pinpoint one particular course of action as a concrete solution to the impending crisis. This means that it is of utmost importance now for the citizens of the world to look towards the future, and not only focus on short-term solutions. How the affected countries will emerge from the upcoming crisis and how the new world will look like are two issues on the agenda that must be addressed with long-term oriented sound money policies. There is still just enough time left for us to bring about the necessary changes that would shape our world in a positive way, making it a better place to live in for us and future generations.

Reference List

Anderson, BM. (1979). *Economics and the Public Welfare: A Financial and Economic History of the United States, 1914-1946*. Indianapolis: Liberty Press.

Artis, MJ. (2002). *Reflections on Optimal Currency Area (OCA) Criteria in the Light of EMU.* Working Paper. Central Bank of Chile.

Athanassiou, P. (2009). *Withdrawal and Expulsion from the EU and EMU – Some Reflections.* ECB Legal Working Paper Series, 10.

Bagus, P. (2007). Asset Prices - An Austrian Perspective. *Procesos de Mercado: Revista Europea de Economía Política* 4(2), 57–93

Bagus, P. (2010). *The Tragedy of the Euro*. Auburn, Ala.: Ludwig von Mises Institute.

Bagus, P. (2016). In Defense of Deflation: A Conversation with Philipp Bagus. *The Austrian* 2(2). March-April 2016.

Bagus, P. and Howden, D. (2011) *Deep Freeze.* Auburn, Ala.: Ludwig von Mises Institute.

Bagus, P. and Schiml, M. (2009). New Modes of Monetary Policy: Qualitative Easing by the Fed. *Economic Affairs*, 29(2), 46-49.

Bank for International Settlements. (2010). *International Banking and Financial Markets Development*. BIS Quarterly Report, 18-22.

Barysch, K. (2010). *Germany, the Euro and the Politics of the Bail-out.* London: Centre for European Reform.

Bastasin, C. (2012). *Saving Europe*. Washington, D.C.: Brookings Institution Press.

Birner, J and Van Zijp, R. (1994). *Hayek, Co-ordination and Evolution: His legacy in Philosophy, Politics, Economics and the History of Ideas*. London: Routledge.

Blanchard, O. (2003). *Macroeconomics.* 3rd ed. Prentice Hall.

Bonner, W. and Addison W. (2003). *Financial Reckoning Day*. Hoboken, N.J.: John Wiley & Sons.

Brown, B. (2010). *Euro Crash*. 2nd ed. Basingstoke: Palgrave Macmillan.

Buiter, W. (2008). *Quantitative and Qualitative Easing: a Terminological and Taxonomic proposal*. [Blog] Times Maverecon Blog. Available at:

http://blogs.ft.com/maverecon/2008/12/quantitative-easing-and-qualitative-easing-a-terminological-and-taxonomic-proposal/ [Accessed 25 May 2016].

Callahan, G. (2006). *Times are Hard: on the Causes of the Business Cycle*. Retrieved: April 30, 2016, from Ludwig von Mises Institute: http://mises.org/daily/2121

Caplin, B. (1997). *Why I am Not an Austrian Economist*. Unpublished Manuscript. Retrieved: April 30, 2016, from: http://econfaculty.gmu.edu/bcaplan/whyaust.htm

Corden, MW. (1972). *Monetary Integration: Essays in International Finance*. Princeton, NJ: Princeton University Press.

Davidson, R. (2013). "Austrian Business Cycle Theory: an Application to New Zealand's Recent Boom and Bust." BBA dissertation. The University of Waikato Management School.

De Soto, JH. (2009). *Money, Bank Credit and Economic Cycles,* 2nd ed. Auburn: Ludwig von Mises Institute.

Doherty, B. (2012). *Ron Paul's Revolution*. New York: Broadside Books.

Ebeling, RM. (1978). *The Austrian Theory of the Trade Cycle*. Center for Libertarian Studies.

Ebeling, RM. (2015). Europe's Move in the Direction of More Monetary Mischief. *Epic Times*, Jan 26, 2015.

Eichengreen, BJ. (2011). *Exorbitant Privilege*. Oxford: Oxford University Press.

European Alliance for Freedom. (2013). *Back to Deutschmark?* Brussels, Belgium.

European Commission. (2002). *Free Movement of Workers: Achieving the Full Benefits and Potential*. Brussels, Belgium: European Commission.

Federal Reserve. (2005). *The Federal Reserve System: Purposes and Functions*. 9th ed.

Fleming, MJ. (1971). On Exchange Rate Unification. *Economic Journal*, 13(26), 467-88.

Guillermo, CA. (1998). Capital Flows and Capital-Market Crises: The Simple Economics of Sudden Stops. *Journal of Applied Economics*, 1, 35-54.

Hammond, JR. (2012). *Ron Paul vs. Paul Krugman*. United States: J.R. Hammond

Hayek, FA. (1976). *Choice in Currency*. London: Institute of Economic Affairs.

Hayek, F., Baxendale, T. and Salerno, J. (2008). *Prices and Production and Other Works*. Auburn, Ala: Ludwig von Mises Institute.

Henkel, H. (2010). *Rettet unser Geld!* Munich: Heyne.

Homburg, S. (1997). *Hat die Waehrungsunion Auswirkungen auf die Finanzpolitik?,* Muenchen: Olzog.

Ingram, JC. (1962). *Regional Payments Mechanisms: the Case of Puerto Rico.* Chapel Hill, NC: University of North Carolina Press.

Jónsson, Á. (2009). *Why Iceland?* New York: McGraw-Hill.

Kenen, PB. (1969). "The Theory of Optimum Currency Areas: An Eclectic View." In *Monetary Problems of the International Economy*, edited by R. Mundell and A. Swoboda. Chicago: University of Chicago Press.

Kim, S. (1998). Economic Integration and Convergence. *Journal of Economic History*, 29(1), 1-32.

Kirzner, IM. (1997). Entrepreneurial Discovery and the Competitive Market Process: An Austrian Approach. *Journal of Economic Literature*, 35, 60-85.

Löffler, K. (2010). *"Paris und London öffnen ihre Archive,"* Ntv.de (November 6, 2010).

Margo, RA. (1998). *Labor Market Integration Before the Civil War.* Working paper, NBER.

Marsh, D. (1992). *The Bundesbank*. London: William Heinemann.

Marsh, D. (2009). *The Euro: the Politics of the New Global Currency.* New Haven, CT: Yale University Press.

Mayer, T. (2012). *Europe's Unfinished Currency*. New York: Anthem Press.

McKinnon, R. (1963). Optimum Currency Areas. *American Economic Review*, 53(4),717-25.

McKinsey & Company, Inc. (2012). *The Future Of The Euro: An Economic Perspective On The Euro Crisis*. McKinsey Germany.

Melitz, MJ. (1996). The Theory of Optimum Currency Areas, Trade and Adjustment. *Open Economics Review* 7(2), 99-116.

Menger, C. (2007). *Principles of Economics.* Auburn, Ala.: Ludwig von Mises Institute. (Original work published in 1871).

Mundell, R. (1961). A Theory of Optimum Currency Areas. *American Economic Review,* 51(3), 657-65.

Murphy, RP. (2016). The Fed Can't Save Us. *The Austrian*, 2(2), 3.

Muth, JF. (1961). Rational Expectations and the Theory of Price Movements. *Econometrica*, 29, 315–335

Organisation for Economic Co-operation and Development. (1999). *EMU: Facts, Challenges and Policies.* Paris: OECD.

Overtveldt, J. (2011). *The End of the Euro*. Chicago: B2 Books.

Parkin M, Powell M & Matthews K. (1997). *Economics.* 3rd ed. Addison-Wesley.

Paul, R. (2008). *The Revolution*. New York: Grand Central Pub.

Paul, R. (2009). *End the Fed.* New York: Grand Central Pub.

Proissl, W. (2010). *Why Germany Fell Out of Love with Europe*. Bruegel Essay and Lecture Series.

Rickards, J. (2011). *Currency Wars*. New York: Portfolio/Penguin.

Rickards, J. (2014). *The Death of Money*. New York: Portfolio/Penguin.

Robbins, L. (1934). *The Great Depression*, London: Macmillan.

Rothbard, M. (1963). *America's Great Depression*. Princeton, N.J.: Van Nostrand.

Rothbard, M. (2009). *Man, Economy and State.* 2nd ed. Auburn, Ala.: Ludwig von Mises Institute. (Original work published in 1962).

Schiff, PD. and Downes, J. (2009). *Crash Proof 2.0*. Hoboken, N.J.: John Wiley.

Schiff, PD. and Schiff, A. (2010). *How an Economy Grows and Why it Crashes*. Hoboken, N.J.: John Wiley.

Smiegel, J. (2010). "Free Movement of Workers in the European Union: Obstacles to EU Labor Mobility and Possibilities to Overcome Them." MA dissertation. Central European University.

Tilford, S. (2006). *Will the Eurozone Crack?* London: Centre for European Reform.

Tommaso, P. (2004). *The Euro and its Central Bank.* Cambridge: MIT Press.

The Economist. (2010). *Charlemagne's Notebook*. May 20, 2010

Tulloch, G. (1988). Why the Austrians are Wrong about Depressions. The *Review of Austrian Economics*, 2,73-78.

Von Haberler, G. (1970). "The International Monetary System: Some Recent Developments and Discussions." In *Approaches to Greater Flexibility in Exchange Rates*, edited by G. Halm. Princeton, NJ: Princeton University Press.

Von Mises, L. (1912). *The Theory of Money and Credit.* Auburn, Ala.: Ludwig von Mises Institute.

Von Mises, L. (1949). *Human Action*. Auburn, Ala.: Ludwig von Mises Institute.

Von Mises, L. (1951). *Inflation: an Unworkable Fiscal Policy*. Auburn, Ala.: Ludwig von Mises Institute.

Varoufakis, Y. (2013). *The Global Minotaur*. London: Zed Books.

Vogt, C. and Leuschel, R. (2011). *The Global Debt Trap*. Hoboken, N.J.: Wiley.

Woods, TE. (2009). *Meltdown*. Washington, DC: Regnery Pub.